PRAISE FOR
Unkind Gifts

"Through personal disclosure of her journey with trauma, Ellen Ranney powerfully captures the jolting, disorienting experience with which any survivor can easily identify. She also provides a theoretical overview, including the latest thinking in neuroscience, to help survivors understand what they go through. On top of all that, she offers a treatment approach that draws from and integrates a wide range of therapies survivors can, as she did, incorporate to turn their traumas into gifts. I think this well-written book is a wonderful resource for trauma survivors."

—Richard Schwartz, PhD
founding developer, Internal Family Systems Therapy and the Center for Self-Leadership

"In this book, Ellen Ranney describes the various theories that inform her understanding of trauma and its impact on those who have been its victims. As she shares her professional perspective, she also weaves in vignettes of her personal experience of trauma and the recovery process. Included in these pages is a great deal of information that others who deal with trauma—whether personally, professionally, or both—may find useful."

—Dorothy S. Becvar, PhD, and Raphael J. Becvar, PhD
authors of *Family Therapy: A Systemic Integration*

Unkind Gifts

AN INSIDER'S GUIDE TO RECOVERY FROM TRAUMA AND LOSS

Unkind Gifts

An Insider's Guide to Recovery from Trauma and Loss

Ellen C. Ranney, PhD

St. Louis

Printed in the United States of America

Bluebird Publishing
St. Louis, Missouri
www.bluebirdpub.com

ISBN: 978-0-9861536-8-6

Cover illustration: Margaret Murphy Schneider
Interior illustrations: Ellen C. Ranney
Book design: Cathy Wood Book Design
Editor: Donna L. Brodsky

For my family
roots, trunk, branches, and twigs

CONTENTS

FOREWORD

In a book published in 2002 by the Young Women's Breast Cancer Program at Washington University School of Medicine in St. Louis, *The Woman Is Stronger Than the Disease: A Guidance Journal for Young Women with Breast Cancer*, Ellen Ranney offered these words of hope and encouragement:

> You will struggle—that is certain—but the struggle can lead you to a place of great strength and insight. I wish you strength and hope on your journey. May the discoveries you make about your place in life lead to great fulfillment for you and those whose lives you touch for many years to come.

As a professor of surgery at the School of Medicine and a member of the team that produced that resource, I had asked Ellen to be a contributor. Four years earlier, Ellen had been diagnosed with breast cancer and had completed a rigorous treatment regimen involving surgery, reconstruction, chemotherapy, and radiation therapy.

When I first met Ellen at the time of her diagnosis, she appeared thoughtful and introspective. She demonstrated a calm that also communicated to me as her physician, "Okay, I understand. What do we do next?" Had I had the chance to read Ellen's book then, I would have recognized that she was experiencing an acute emotional trauma.

As a longtime professor of surgery at a major academic medical center with a National Cancer Institute designation, I knew the impact of each individual diagnosis was poignant and personal. Like most breast surgical oncologists, I maintained the role of professional, attempting to provide the very best in a somewhat scientific explanation of the diagnosis of breast cancer, treatment options, expected course, and outcome. And like many other breast surgeons, I developed a professional but nonetheless very real affection for most of my patients, as I did with Ellen. But also like most of my colleagues, despite the years of experience that had made me a confident professional, I did not necessarily deal with my patients' inner turmoil and fear.

As a professional caregiver, I was unaware of the ongoing effects of this sort of trauma on patients. But *Unkind Gifts*—which examines emotional trauma as an entity affecting human development and subsequent recovery—has shined a bright light on what my patients are going through. Today, armed with the insights on the psychological, physical, and emotional impact of breast cancer that *Unkind Gifts* provides, I am much better equipped to accompany my patients on their journeys. It is my sincere hope that my colleagues will read this book to truly understand the impact of the maladies we treat.

Unkind Gifts is equally a "must read" for victims of trauma. Ellen's organized, thoughtful approach to healing blends established psychologic principles with a poignant, personal story of her own reactions of grief, anger, uncertainty, and fear around the diagnosis of breast cancer. In her book, Ellen explains the importance of feeling, listening, and being open to the traumatic occurrence, emphasizing the importance of "witnessing" emotions. She offers suggestions for increasing self-awareness, self-expression, and acceptance through breathing exercises, art and movement practices, mindfulness, and psychotherapy. Ellen also describes an array of interventions and practices that allowed her to integrate her feelings while moving forward on her road to recovery. As a practitioner of "Western medicine" and a fierce defender of data-driven therapies, I found the section on the chakras system of Hindu spiritualists among the most enlightening and optimistic.

Perhaps most important, in addressing the critical roles of professional and nonprofessional supporters, Ellen advises readers that mindfulness-based psychotherapy provides an effective means to achieve recovery, giving the person who has experienced trauma the permission and encouragement to seek help and guidance from experienced professionals.

This work is not one woman's anecdote; if you are seeking a magic solution or a quick fix, this book is not for you. Rather, this is an exceptional rendering of trauma, loss, healing, and recovery. Although told from the perspective of a breast cancer survivor, *Unkind Gifts* will speak to anyone who has suffered emotional trauma. It is based in scientific fact and told with incredible personal perspective, providing encouragement, guidance, and proof that the effort to identify and deal with trauma and loss will surely be rewarded by self-awareness and peace.

You have in your hands a precious gift from a survivor who is also an experienced, committed, and compassionate therapist. Open your mind to this book's teachings and your heart to Ellen's experience. Both will guide you on your own path to healing.

Virginia Herrmann, MD
Washington University School of Medicine
in St. Louis

PREFACE

Trauma is an unkind gift, a double-edged sword. The sharp edges of this sword destroy an individual's expectations of safety and uproot prior supports, leaving the sufferer emotionally adrift. But it is this very stripping-down to basics that provides the space for the emergence of new coping abilities and makes it possible to build new resources. Like an iron sword, people are tempered and tested by trauma. This testing can either break those who experience trauma or help them become stronger and wiser for the effort exerted.

I came to this realization several years after I was diagnosed with breast cancer in 1998. Almost twenty years before this "epiphany," when I began working with trauma survivors in a substance abuse program in 1983, I didn't see trauma as an unkind gift. In the early 1990s, when I started seeing victims of childhood sexual abuse in my psychotherapy practice, that concept was still unknown to me—though I was determined to offer a supportive environment to help those trauma survivors heal. Even, and especially, when I was diagnosed with breast cancer, I thought the well-meaning strangers who called my diagnosis a "gift" were merely using platitudes to manage their own anxieties, trying to reassure themselves that I could somehow benefit from this dreaded diagnosis so they could more easily go about their own lives.

Not until many years later, as my cancer experience became more distant and I regained a sense of relative "safety," did I begin to recognize how exposure to trauma can give survivors an edge. Having been there myself and having recovered, I realized that from the painful place of trauma, it becomes possible for the survivor to gain a hard-won, new perspective or "insider tip": although trauma is inevitably unkind, recovery is not only possible but may be rich with discovery and opportunities for grace.

In my case, the greatest gift I was fortunate to attain in the wake of my trauma was renewed health—despite the necessary adaptations to my missing and rearranged body parts and the limitations imposed by repeated, toxic treatments of chemotherapy and radiation. But another gift, beyond renewed health, was my new-found ability to not "sweat the small stuff," profoundly differentiating my after-cancer life from my before-cancer existence.

This second gift changed the framework of my habitual point of view, setting the stage for a host of new discoveries of well-being. The years of pushing myself past the point of exhaustion to keep up with imagined and unsustainable standards of productivity were over; my priorities shifted to attending to my body and responding to cues of fatigue or imbalance. Instead of relying on external standards of achievement and beauty, and striving to perform according to what I imagined as others' judgments of my worth, I consciously chose kindness toward myself for my best intentions and inherent value. I still adhere to this perspective today, more than seventeen years after my diagnosis.

*****

Unkind Gifts is the story of a journey through the world of trauma recovery as I experienced it personally and have learned over the years from other survivors. Once I was diagnosed with breast cancer, my surgery was scheduled. It was set only five days after the long-planned licensing exam that would qualify me to be a full-fledged psychotherapist. That's how trauma generally arrives: unexpectedly and without invitation. Sudden and overwhelming, trauma takes away all familiar landmarks and leaves us in a strange new land with no sense of direction.

Despite my disorientation, I was fortunate to have many models on which to base my survival efforts. Credit for my physical survival goes to the miracles of modern medicine, but my recovery has been the work of many teachers, most importantly the ones I found within. Clients had already shown me that it is possible to arise anew from even the worst of tragedies; practitioners of alternative and complementary healing supported me and offered guidance as I forged my own individual path; and family and friends gathered near and cheered me on.

Traveling this path has privileged me to meet many others on their own similar but unique pilgrimages toward trauma recovery. None of us has a map, but the sharing of stories and time spent searching has allowed me to cobble together a set of directions—a sort of compass to orient myself and others to the path.

*****

Many books offer valuable technical information about trauma treatment; others relate sensational stories of painful traumatic histories. Precious few address the practical challenges of finding a way through the recovery process and shine a light down that path.

To offer a clear view of the emotional challenges of this shared journey, I have used my own experience with breast cancer as the "case study." A journal entry with personal reflections on my cancer experience sets up each of the ten chapters. Before and after each journal entry is a drawing or painting that illustrates and reinforces the takeaways that I hope survivors, their caregivers, and their families will glean. Additional stories of lessons that I learned from my clients and my own interactions with friends and family, as well as from my "internal family" of Parts, appear throughout the book.

Readers who wish information beyond that presented in this book's ten chapters will find two appendixes. In appendix A are ideas to help professionals assist trauma survivors. Appendix B offers support for family members and other partners in relational healing.

I have spent seventeen years, and a lifetime, finding my way through greater and lesser traumas, and I am only beginning to grasp what I have been given. Awareness of these gifts is what I have attempted to share in this book. It is my fondest hope that others' journeys will pick up where mine leaves off, so those traveling behind me can benefit from the collective wisdom of shared healing.

*****

I am deeply grateful to the many clients and friends who shared their experiences of recovery with me, and to the many doctors, therapists, and body workers who gave of their healing resources during my recovery. My sincere thanks go to Dick Schwartz for his amazing and generous model, and for the hope it continues to offer me and all others who have suffered from loss.

The advice, support, and guidance of many individuals was invaluable to me as I developed, drafted, and refined this book. Special thanks are due to Jenna Mueller, who read early drafts and provided important encouragement, and to Marian Sandmaier, who advised me on the book's structure and organization. My dear friend Jean Caine introduced me to Interpersonal Neurobiology and has shared her compassion and enthusiasm for work with trauma survivors; many of the suggestions I offer here are inspired by my discussions with Jean. For their guidance in transforming my manuscript, journal entries, and artwork into book format, I am grateful to Dan Thompson, Donna Brodsky, and Cathy Wood at Bluebird Publishing.

To my husband, Elliott, and my sons, Bryan, Stephen, and Will—who traveled this long road with me, supported me, and inspired and encouraged me—I owe eternal gratitude; you have my unending love. And, finally, I thank my siblings, who continue to provide lessons in loyalty, keeping the spirit of our loved ones lit between us.

THE FIRST PART

GETTING STARTED

The first part of this book serves as a foundation for understanding the influence of emotional trauma on human development. The lens through which this influence can be seen most effectively is that of attachment theory, a model of relationship structure arising from childhood experiences.

As chapter one points out, our sense of who we are and whether we can manage difficulties in our lives is established within patterns of early attachment. If a child's basic emotional needs are not met, the resulting developmental trauma will affect relationships throughout their life.

Chapter two explores the disruptions to healthy attachment wrought by the trauma of abuse and neglect. Whether from such early relationship struggles or from profound experiences of terror and loss in later life, trauma is difficult to process. If information related to traumatic loss is left unprocessed indefinitely, disruptions emerge in the form of emotional reactivity to reminders of the original event. By knowing what we needed that was either unavailable or lost, we can take the first step in the trauma recovery process toward a sense of competency and self-worth.

Chapter three offers insight into discovering the energy of our core self. Trauma and neglect seem to communicate an inability to manage things, blocking us from accessing our genuine and worthy essence. But guided by the elements of secure attachment, we can clear away those blocks, access the Self-energy needed to shore up our foundations, and create new support structures for current and future relationships.

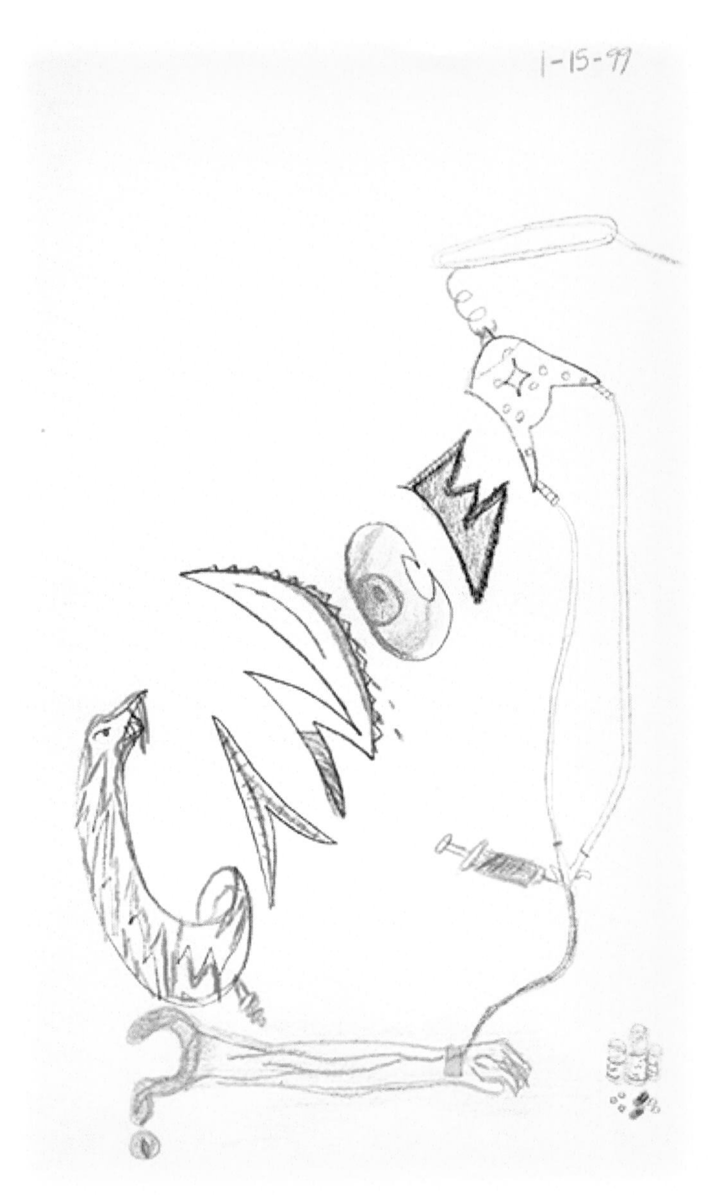

A diagnosis of cancer brings with it many fearful imaginings—
and many frightening realities.

one

SHAPING A SELF

Unkind Gifts

It was a feeling like falling, like someone had pushed me backwards from the top of a long staircase only recently climbed. My sense of disorientation was profound, and I was struggling to grab the railing to catch myself before it was too late, before I ended up huddled in a heap at the foot of the stairs, unable to rise again.

That was the sensation I experienced even as I sat in a chair next to my husband, holding his hand and hearing, "First of all, the left breast is perfect." It was the "good news/bad news" form of delivery. This attentive, caring doctor I had only just met was trying so hard to be kind. But I was in big trouble. I had cancer.

As I tightened my grip on Elliott's hand, everything seemed in slow motion. The doctor described the tiny little dots on the mammogram as microcalcifications, precancerous milk ducts, and the lump on the side of my right breast as a probable malignancy. Down the hall, in a cold room full of technicians running a variety of electromechanical devices, they put me on a table with a hole in it to allow my right breast to hang through. While they poked, prodded, and clamped that suddenly foreign part of my anatomy, all I could think of was a cow at milking time. My sense of estrangement from myself increased the longer I stayed in that awkward position, with strangers in white coats arranging and discussing me.

Hours later, I was finally back home—feeling relieved one moment, terrified the next. My body—which I had groomed and nurtured and exploited and depended on for so long—had turned against me. The offending breast was numb and seemed disconnected from the rest of me, not just because of the ice pack and pain meds. There was no place safe anymore; I was a stranger in a strange land. My surroundings seemed unfamiliar, even though I was in my own home.

I called the people I trusted most, but even they couldn't help me. I had always been the strong one, the family manager. I kept wanting to apologize for letting them down.

I spent long, sleepless nights clinging to Elliott as if he was a life raft in a sea of sharks and jellyfish while I silently counted the months and years to various milestones in my children's lives. My boys were so young—only sixteen, thirteen, and eight—far too young to take on this terrible burden.

"In ten years," I thought to myself, "the boys will be through high school. But how long will I have to live to be a grandmother—even for a little while? What if I don't make it? How will they manage without me? Will Elliott be able to rise to the many occasions that make up a normal life?"

Nothing in my oh-so-fortunate lifetime had prepared me for this challenge—not my caring family, not my degree in counseling, not my practice in trauma therapy. Nothing. I could stand outside myself, watching the sudden dread and the startle reflex that comes with the trauma response. "So that's what it really feels like," I thought.

Once you've experienced trauma,
it's hard to feel safe ever again.

Let's face it: we're all survivors of something. We may have grown up chanting, "Sticks and stones can break my bones, but words will never hurt me." But the truth is, how we're spoken to and treated by others can have lasting effect.

—ꟿ—

How we're spoken to and treated by others can have lasting effect.

—ꟿ—

Emotional abuse shapes our identity; neglect becomes a perpetual state when lessons from childhood are taken in as indicators of all we are or can ever hope to be. Our developmental story may include experiences and meanings that are gentle and benign, or days of hurt and confusion that seem to dominate who we are. In any case, there are inevitable losses that shake us to our core; of such are human relationships made.

Those moments when we feel out of control shape our expectations and responses, at times leaving us profoundly changed at a level of meaning-making—an existential level that informs our ability to cope and move forward in life. Changing and challenging those roles is like swimming against a strong current, likely one that we unknowingly help create and maintain by our very belief that how we've been treated is who we are.

Some people seem to ride these rough seas and emerge stronger; but others are left feeling damaged and hopeless. It's common to look at others and compare our stories to theirs, as if there were a direct ratio of pain to coping that we're all equally capable of adhering to. Each of us, however, carries a unique blueprint from our own early relationships that defines our sense of identity in adulthood. And a key element in establishing that blueprint is the model of self that arises from the responsiveness, or unresponsiveness, of caregivers to our expressed needs in our first months of life.

THE ROLE OF ATTACHMENT

It is difficult to understand what goes wrong in traumatic situations without first knowing what "going right" looks like. Research into human development led to a central idea for understanding and tracking early lessons in personal worth and expectations within relationships: the "working model of self," developed by John Bowlby.[1] This attachment-based model—drawn from interactions with caregivers within the context of day-to-day attention to an infant's needs for nurturance and soothing—establishes a child's expectations for all future relationships.

Studying childcare practices in an orphanage, Bowlby observed that although the infants received enough food and attention to their basic physical needs, they were seldom picked up, held, or related to emotionally. He also noticed a high rate of infant mortality in these orphanages, as well as a failure to thrive on the part of the children. Bowlby concluded that these little ones were dying because they lacked comfort and security—attachment.

Bowlby's work was taken up and extended in 1978 in a ground-breaking study, "the strange situation," which remains central to our understanding of attachment even today.[2] In this study, toddlers were observed individually during a series of events that began with their mother leaving them alone in a room. Once the child was alone, a stranger entered and quickly left the room; then, the mother returned. The toddlers' reactions to reuniting with their mothers were observed and scored along a range from secure (able to calm and reconnect) to insecure (showing continued reactivity or acting out).

Based on the concept that caregiver responses create a "mirror" through which a child's identity is shaped, attachment theory has been applied to explain much of human behavior. Thanks in large part to Bowlby's early work, we know that patterns of attachment that are established in early childhood—whether secure or insecure—become lasting characteristics of relationships into both adulthood and next-generation parenting.

Let me be clear that insecure attachment is not necessarily due to parental "failures." There are many influences in a child's development and many challenges in parenting—not least of which is the larger issue of social support. Families may lack access to necessary resources, perhaps pulling energy and attention away from a child's needs. And a parent will inevitably have to spend time away from the child, potentially facing conflicts in areas such as family support, finances, health, and social inequities. In some families, illness or other special needs may create seemingly impossible dilemmas, leaving them barely coping with one crisis after another.

It is difficult for even the most fortunate of us to achieve the ideal balance of "good enough" parenting.[3] Attachment influences go far beyond the range of what any individual parent can assume full responsibility for. And it is important to note that attachment is not a one-way process: infant temperament influences the "fit" between parent and child, further shaping patterns of interaction.[4]

SECURE ATTACHMENT

A parent who is engaged and attuned to the distress signals of a newborn baby will try a range of options to calm that distress. From this beginning emerges in the child a set of finely tuned monitoring skills for responding to signals across the spectrum of human emotions. But parental responsiveness does more than address the needs of the infant. Equally important, it offers both the parent and the child a sense of competence and increased satisfaction, bonding the two in a lifelong partnership of meaning and connectedness.

Attuned relationships between parent and child take place on a continuum of care across generations, establishing expectations around worth, competence, and purpose for the developing person. Early experiences of secure attachment become enduring patterns with lasting implications for adult relationships and parenting into future generations. Such attuned models of response are a source of lasting emotional well-being and powerfully influence options for recovery from the inevitable losses and disruptions that are a normal part of life.

INSECURE ATTACHMENT

Insecure attachment has three main forms[5]:

- **Avoidant/dismissive attachment** is characterized by the parent's distant or disinterested attention to the child's basic needs for nurturance and affection. This pattern of neglect mirrors to the child that they are unworthy and that life is beyond their capacity to control. Emotional restriction and lack of depth of feeling in relationships are a child's likely responses to this parenting pattern. Mr. Spock, the logic-driven Vulcan in "Star Trek," exhibits an extreme case of avoidant attachment disorder.

- In **anxious/preoccupied attachment**, the parent surrenders emotional management of the relationship to the child, communicating fear and incompetence in a big, frightening world. This parenting style often leaves the child disabled by doubt and dependency. As a result, the child's later relationships may be colored by anxiety and resentment.
- **Disorganized/unclassified attachment** is a catch-all category for dysfunctional parenting that includes abuse, exploitation of the child's vulnerabilities, and neglect of the child's emotional needs. This type of environment severely undermines a child's trust in self and others, and can result in mental illness, dissociative disorders, or other extreme disruptions of development. For the child, the only way to survive in this environment often is to either join in the chaos or "check out" indefinitely.

Among these three categories of suboptimal attachment are greater and lesser examples of victimization, and reduced coping resources—often the precursors to recurring traumatic exposure and post-traumatic stress.

ATTACHMENT TRAUMA

In their positive mode, mechanisms of attachment offer a sense of security and allow us to view the world as manageable. Experiencing a strong foundation within the primary relationships of early childhood therefore makes it more likely that an individual can successfully negotiate interpersonal challenges throughout life. When out-of-the-norm events arise—sometimes referred to as "little-t traumas"[6] of grief and hurt—we are not emotionally stalled. Secure interpersonal relationships also offer an internalized place for the individual to recover from "big-T traumas" such as severe illness, sudden loss, victimization, or natural disasters.

But what if the process fails due to disruptions of parenting or family support? When the developmental environment is less than optimal—through illness, loss, neglect, or abandonment—these early lessons "stick" no less thoroughly, and the individual's sense of self as worthy and competent is undermined.

A child who experiences a lack of, or loss of, appropriately responsive parenting is affected for life. When basic human needs for security and nurturing are not met, a pattern is laid down within the nervous system to accommodate to the unmet need. Relationship choices and life expectations, as well as self-care and, ultimately, parenting skills, are inevitably disrupted.

Growing up in a home where depression or substance abuse blocks the needed connection with a loving and attentive parent, children may miss out on important emotional stimulation, leaving them to accommodate to the gaps through their own efforts. With no clear guidance, kids learn to self-soothe through temporary or maladaptive means. Self-destructive or violent behavior may become the substitute, especially since kids often see the world from an egocentric, it-must-be-my-fault point of view.

Even more extreme is the situation where a child's efforts to engage with others are met with abuse. Through what can only be the more powerful person's choice, a developing child is punished for their very vulnerability—severely distorting the child's sense of self and expectations for future relationships.

Insecure attachment patterns, although initially adaptive to the developmental environment, tend to result in reduced options for coping and lowered self-worth, factoring heavily into adult relationships. These less attuned response patterns by impaired adult caregivers are considered "adverse childhood experiences."[7] Such experiences often lead to an increased likelihood of negative coping and less effective decision making in life—carrying toxic stress into future relationships, disrupting immune functioning, shaping the nervous system, and affecting other physical and emotional factors of health and well-being.

NEW PERSPECTIVES ON RECOVERY

Although our destiny is in many respects tied to our attachment history, recent discoveries in interpersonal neurobiology hold new promise for the possibility of lasting change.[8] It was previously thought that the workings of attachment were set early in life and couldn't be easily adapted later. But thanks to new technology for studying the brain, we now know that early attachment patterns can be successfully reshaped by interpersonally attuned responsiveness.

Until the turn of the millennium, indirect approaches to change, such as talk therapies, dominated the field of mental health. Talk therapies often led to some sort of change, but what was actually happening to promote that change was left mostly to conjecture.

A call for more "efficacy-based" tools led to heavy reliance on cognitive therapies emphasizing how we think as a way to manage what we feel. Considered "top-down" approaches, cognitively focused therapies often result in behavioral change, but they may stop short of true emotional recovery. New options that have proved effective in the healing process have arisen from an unexpected direction: from the bottom up.

How Healing Happens

On the journey to healing after exposure to trauma and loss, the victim must not turn away from or ignore emotions and behaviors but instead must witness them with compassion. Change comes about not through intervention by an outside force, but through the supportive attention, responsive caring, and witnessing energy of the self. Then, the individual's "working model" can be modified and expanded though this new awareness and representation of needs and choices, and the outdated model can be reset to a new, more functional version.

Powerful emotions that might overwhelm our ability to cope in the midst of a life-altering, life-threatening event are contained in a primal area of the brain, the amygdala. The amygdala sits where the brain stem (the road to the body) joins the neo-cortex of the brain (the site of executive function). This temporary storage arrangement is incredibly effective for survival, since to react to intense terror in the moment of traumatic occurrence might block available escape options or may lead to increased harm. However, when temporary emotional holding becomes long-term practice, the trauma-based material tends to cycle through at inopportune moments, seeking resolution but disrupting the survivor's ongoing emotional development.

Due to their unprocessed state, these experiences feel as though they are occurring in the present, "stuck in time." But through calm exploration by the individual, either alone or supported by a psychotherapist, these events and emotional responses can be moved to the hippocampus. In this walnut-size brain area, the experiences can begin to be processed and a perspective of time factored in, diminishing the ongoing sense of threat.

The task of completing unprocessed emotional material then becomes possible through telling one's story, knowing one's own truth, and eventually storing what was a present moment–seeming threat as a memory of past hurt. Information is then integrated via the midbrain (medial cortex) and made available at a cognitive level for decision making, so actions can more effectively be directed toward resolution and safety.

Mindfulness

Mindfulness-based practices have emerged as the "new" road to recovery from trauma, one that reaches back to ancient spiritual traditions of meditation and breath focus. Initially considered merely a noninvasive way to cope with what cannot be changed, mindfulness now is used widely in therapy offices and hospital treatment centers. Along with an awareness of the importance of relationships in human development and healing, and the inclusion of body-work, mindfulness practices increasingly have a mainstream role in emotional and physical recovery.

Unlike "top-down," cognitively based psychotherapy, mindful therapies offer a "bottom-up" process that promotes healing through the practice of internal awareness, which opens new pathways and clears blocked energies. The brain naturally adapts, shifting focus and energy. So healing becomes a multilevel, holistic process, offering improved self-worth, greater acceptance, and improved immune functioning.

One way to track recovery is by looking at the functioning of the autonomic nervous system (ANS). The ANS is composed of two processes of adaptive functioning: sympathetic and parasympathetic. The sympathetic nervous system, with its connection to heart and lungs, can be viewed as a revving motor that often gets overcharged in our complex, stressful society. Stress on the body releases adrenaline, which is destructive to muscle tissue and organs. The counter-balancing parasympathetic nervous system, which is needed to recover and recharge for the next task, becomes harder to engage as it struggles to bring the body back to neutral.

This "open-throttle" way of coping becomes dangerous over time, especially for those who grow up in insecure attachment environments. A common coping tool for trauma victims is hypervigilance: the mind and body constantly monitor the environment for threats, leaving few resources for managing any additional stressors that arise. Weakened immune systems and damaged organs are common among those who have experienced trauma.

The combined effects of exposure to pollution, stress, and limited opportunity for "down time" create a vicious cycle in Western societies. Among those affected by trauma, the cycle is exacerbated by feelings of helplessness and loss of control. The sympathetic nervous system quickly adapts to demands for an ever-increasing output of energy; but simultaneously, we become less able to attend to recovery in a calm, centered way.

Centering is crucial to bring the parasympathetic nervous system back online to reduce stress and to decrease demands on the heart and other essential organs. But calm is not easily accessed in our busy, information-packed society, which takes a toll on us all. The resulting loss of energy and health contributes further to feelings of helplessness and hopelessness, leaving those affected by trauma even more wounded and worn.

When we take time to breathe and center our attention—to practice mindfulness—our hearts stop racing with fear and expectations. Then we can engage in real time, where fearful thoughts and old regrets take a back seat to present-moment awareness. This practice brings the mind to a calm center, opening the brain to new understandings—rather than expecting this moment, this person, or this event to be just like past examples.

When we breathe and center our attention, our hearts stop racing with fear and expectations.

A calm center is like the brain of a newborn in its receptivity, though still structured by life experience. From this new perspective, we can see things from a less judgmental point of view. Even long-ago attachment models can be accessed and changed to access healthier relationship skills. Through such compassionate awareness, opportunities for revising expectations and responses arise, allowing the mind and body to calm and heal, and the future to unfold.

Notes

1. John Bowlby, *Attachment: Attachment and Loss*, vol. 1 (New York: Basic Books, 1969), 210–30.

2. Mary D. Salter Ainsworth, Mary C. Blehar, Everett Waters, and Sally N. Wall, eds., *Patterns of Attachment: A Psychological Study of the Strange Situation* (Hillsdale, NJ: Erlbaum, 1978), 287–94.

3. Donald W. Winnicott, *The Child, the Family, and the Outside World* (London: Middlesex, 1973), 69–74.

4. Stella Chess and Alexander Thomas, *Temperament in Clinical Practice* (New York: Guilford, 1986), 51–62.

5. Mary Main, "The Organized Categories of Infant, Child, and Adult Attachment: Flexible vs. Inflexible Attention Under Attachment-Related Stress," *Journal of the American Psychoanalytic Association*, no. 48 (2000):1055–95.

6. Judith Lewis Herman, *Trauma and Recovery: The Aftermath of Violence—from Domestic Abuse to Political Terror* (New York: Basic Books, 1992), 115–29.

7. Centers for Disease Control and Prevention, "Adverse Childhood Experiences Study," 2008. Available at http://www.cdc.gov/nccdogo/ace/.

8. Daniel J. Siegel, *The Developing Mind: Toward a Neurobiology of Interpersonal Experience* (New York: Guilford, 1999), 3–28.

Who decides how you will move forward?

two

UNDERSTANDING TRAUMA AND LOSS

Rough Cut

My new breast was an ugly purple mound, but the doctors kept saying how good it looked. Bandages covered my torso, and drains hung from several incisions, steadily filling with evil-looking liquid. I felt like I'd been taken apart, then reassembled with a few pieces missing.

As the effects of the anesthetic subsided, I thought about the fiasco of the day before surgery, my thirty-ninth birthday; it had felt much like I imagined it would to attend my own wake. My birthday lunch had featured my parents and seven of my eight siblings. I was the first member of my family to face a potentially life-threatening illness, and fear and pity showed in all their eyes. I tried to contain my own anxiety but had a hard time doing so.

My desire had been to spend that ironically awful birthday collecting my thoughts and energies to prepare for the roller coaster ride to follow. Working at supporting a healing attitude, I attended my regular early morning yoga class.

As the class got underway, I was dismayed to see that my sister Jane, my usual yoga companion, was absent. I knew she viewed being there as important because she had been with me at my doctor appointments, discussing options, and crying with me ever since my diagnosis. I became more and more concerned, struggling to avoid distraction and follow the class routine.

When we were in the final relaxation pose—ironically, the "corpse pose"—a desk attendant in clicking heels came into the gymnasium. There was whispering between the attendant and the instructor, but the sibilant sound of "sister, sister" was all I heard.

My knees gave way when, the class ended, the instructor walked over to tell me the news: my sister had been carjacked in the fitness center's parking lot. She quickly assured me that Jane was OK and hustled me to the office to collect myself to call her. But as we turned the corner, my sister was walking toward us. We both burst into tears and threw our arms around one another. She was still frightened, but unhurt, and had lost her purse and car; she didn't want to upset everyone by mentioning the gun that her attacker had brandished. For a few moments, I had no thoughts about my surgery the next day.

At the birthday party, everyone tried to be upbeat, but the mood was somber and anxious. Jane's carjacking crisis was discussed, then swept aside, returning me to my earlier sense of foreboding of the next day. I somehow managed to eat cake and open the large assortment of "sick-person" gifts from my anxious parents and siblings: pajamas, slippers, new sheets—all the while wishing that I could go to sleep for the next six months or so.

* * * * *

On the morning of the surgery, I felt relief: my sense of anticipation and dread would finally be over. Or would it? There would be many hurdles ahead—and no hope of returning to "how life had been" since my new status as a cancer victim would always be with me.

I told the boys good-bye, knowing it would be several days before my return, trying to put on a happy face for them. Once in the car with my equally fearful husband, I mentally said "good riddance" to the tumor and "goodbye, old friend" to the body parts soon to be lost.

After the surgery, I heard a voice asking me to move my feet. Then, bright lights flashed overhead. I wished silently that my gurney would stop bumping around so I could go back to sleep. I heard my mother's worried voice, remarking how pale I looked.

When I awoke later, my mother was sitting near me, holding my hand and saying with a mix of fear and relief, "There you are!" In my profound vulnerability, still tainted with uncertainty and the effects of anesthesia, she seemed to me to be my only link to safety. I wished I were still small enough to climb into her lap so she could rock me protectively in her arms.

* * * * *

The next days were morphine blurred: sleeping and waking to find a different person in my room, and an endless parade of doctors and nurses. An attentive family member was nearby twenty-four hours a day to help me drink water or adjust my covers, to chat quietly in the dark about what was going on outside my narrow little world, and to keep me from feeling so alone.

When the boys came to visit, I was relieved to see them. But seeing the looks on their faces, I wondered if it had been a bad idea for them to come. Their shocked expressions reflected the new reality: their formerly composed, in-charge, competent mother was in an altered state. Clearly, this experience would leave all of us changed.

Even when you have moved away from the trauma, life events have a way of taking you back to the same sense of pain and confusion. Suddenly, it feels as if you have to start the journey to recovery all over again.

Traumatic events can be life-threatening, "big-T" situations, such as military combat or large-scale natural disasters, or subtle but chronic exposures to danger, as might occur in a neglectful or abusive home. A range of extreme experiences can happen to people—leaving some with difficulty moving on or with symptoms of post-traumatic stress disorder (PTSD)[1] while others are seemingly unphased.

By contrast, life transitions or occurrences that might be "little-t" traumas, easily resolved in most people—for example, the death of a beloved pet or a close friend's move to another city—can cause lasting pain to others. Even those who seem unphased in the aftermath of a "little-t" trauma, however, may discover that such events shape their expectations of negative outcomes in the future.

To try to manage their overwhelming confusion, many who experience trauma blame themselves—and in so doing become increasingly vulnerable to destructive coping and dysfunctional relationships. Self-blame is especially associated with losses early in life, experiences that are compounded by complicated developmental environments, or by a series of traumatic events over time. For example, a parent's job loss, with accompanying financial strain, may affect a child's opportunity to engage in after-school activities. In this context, bullying comments by the child's peers might become imbued with greater intensity, leaving the victimized child feeling hopeless and desperate for escape, even in self-destructive ways. These compounded "little t's" can escalate rapidly, leading to a full-blown post-traumatic response.

THE TRAUMA RESPONSE

When events overwhelm our ability to cope, we may find ourselves reacting automatically in a behavioral pattern that has come to be known as the trauma response. At the core of this response is a profound experience of lost security in an unpredictable world.

In the wake of severe trauma, trust—the most basic of developmental tasks[2]—is disrupted at nearly every level of human interaction: the environment, the body, relationships, and even our spiritual base. No place seems safe from threat; no person seems likely to care. Factors like gender, appearance, intelligence, decision-making ability, and human vulnerability become objects of misplaced blame, alienating the victim from his own physical being.

The timing and consistency of the caregiver's response to a child's need for nurturance and protection sets the stage for all future relationships. The resulting balance of "trust vs. mistrust" establishes our sense of the world as either a safe environment where our needs will be addressed or a hostile place demanding constant vigilance against threat. If the primary developmental "crisis" of trust is poorly managed, future relationships will be compromised by the lack of a strong foundation.

Disruptions to trust can occur later in life as well, creating lasting expectations of loss. Experiences of sudden traumatic loss can block our existing sense of safety, leaving us waiting for the proverbial "other shoe" to drop.

Whether due to childhood maltreatment or sudden loss in adulthood, victims of trauma suffer violation at a primary level of trust, resulting in a tendency to draw inward to protect the self from further pain. This need for self-protection can lead sufferers to cut off relationships out of a sense of futility or feeling like a burden—even to push away supportive friends to feel more in control of what they view as inevitable abandonment and loss.

Victims of trauma suffer violation at a primary level of trust.

By contrast, trauma victims may become so dependent on their supporters that they nearly choke the life out of those relationships—pushing boundaries, demanding reassurance, and challenging loyalties to a point that overwhelms even the most patient and loyal friends and loved ones. This "self-protective" coping may block access to real healing, establishing a continuing pattern of self-perpetuating "betrayal."

What Is PTSD?

Post-traumatic stress disorder (PTSD) was first recognized in combat veterans in the late twentieth century. The diagnosis was soon noted for its application to other survivors of trauma and abuse. However, its inconsistent appearance among those who have been exposed to the same event has challenged trauma professionals in diagnosing the condition and identifying the best approaches to treatment.

For PTSD sufferers, a huge challenge is to understand their own reactions to out-of-control life experiences. Most symptoms of PTSD reflect efforts to control the environment—by either rigid management of rules and boundaries (sometimes to an obsessive level) or a chaotic display of reactions to even the slightest reminders of the trauma ("triggers"). It is common, for example, for trauma victims to demand that support persons adhere rigidly to meeting times or return phone calls immediately, regardless of the supporter's own schedule or responsibilities. PTSD sufferers also may display extreme reactions to certain words or phrases that remind them of the traumatic experience. Such demanding and unpredictable behavior can cause even the most devoted supporter to burn out, creating a self-fulfilling prophecy of abandonment in the trauma survivor's life.

The trauma sufferer's demanding,
unpredictable behavior
can cause even the most devoted
supporter to burn out.

Because of the way trauma affects the central nervous system, trauma sufferers may find themselves distanced from their emotions at some times but at other times trapped in expectations of imminent danger. Feelings of emotional numbness countered by anxiety-based intrusions and "flashbacks" of the traumatic event, are defining characteristics of PTSD. When the details of traumatic events are unconsciously held or are kept secret due to shame, the victim can find it highly confusing and counterproductive to think or talk about such events, reinforcing the sense of helplessness and hopelessness of the original trauma. Such natural coping mechanisms, although functional at the time of the traumatic occurrence, may later block access to opportunities for healing.

Who can blame the trauma victim—lacking any sense of the possibility for positive change—for "taking cover"? The pressure to give in to an overwhelming sense of hopelessness can be intense for victims and helpers alike. For this reason, a professional support system can be essential to help survivors—and their families—find a way to the new normal.

Dissociation

When we experience events that are too overwhelming to be endured—especially childhood experiences of betrayal or when we are powerless to escape intense pain—our nervous system protectively blocks our awareness to allow continued functioning. This natural process, essential to survival in extremely dangerous situations, is called dissociation. Dissociation offers the trauma victim a chance to function for a while without the looming presence and pain of traumatic loss.

Repeated exposure to traumatic events from an early age can lead to extremes of dissociation: disconnecting to the point of not knowing our own experiences or feelings. Such sensory blocks may include the inability to recall part or all of an event (amnesia) and a temporary inability to feel physical pain (analgesia).

Even long after a traumatic event, the physical and emotional sense of risk can be nearly overwhelming for the trauma survivor, causing the brain to fire orders to the body's endocrine system in preparation for action that may never have opportunity for release.[3] Contemplating ordinary tasks—like entering a crowded mall to do some shopping, much less taking the even more frightening risk of attempting connection with another person—can lead to numbing dissociation.

In dissociated trauma, emotional pain isn't processed, so it can't be stored effectively as memory. Instead, elements of the trauma are separated into component parts and held below the surface of awareness. Although this may provide the trauma victim a temporary respite, thoughts and situations can trigger the reemergence of the traumatic experience, setting off alarms, overloading the sufferer's mind and body ("intrusion"), and shutting down ("numbing") the system.

Dissociation exists on a continuum from mild ("spacing out") to extreme (separately functioning "personalities"). Some survivors turn to drugs and alcohol to create or maintain dissociation, "self-medicating" to block memories and emotional pain. Other self-destructive behaviors like cutting, eating disorders, sexual acting out, and overspending are also based in dissociative coping. But these addictive processes only add further problems to the mix, causing increasing strain on the survivor's body, mind, and relationships.

The longer it is necessary for the sufferer to put off addressing the consequences of the trauma—whether due to a lack of resources or an inability to seek help because of continued threat (as in a war zone or an abusive environment)—the more likely it is that dissociative coping will become a primary means of managing emotional challenges. Once dissociation is ingrained, it becomes a trap from which escape is very difficult.

CHALLENGES IN TRAUMA RECOVERY

Trauma recovery is an ongoing effort. Even after many years have passed, the survivor may continue to be reminded of times of fear and vulnerability, which seem to be occurring in the present moment. But with effective internal and external supports, trauma triggers can be negotiated. By exploring meanings and engaging present-moment experiences, the survivor can counter old expectations around continued destructive patterns and engage new relationship skills in their stead.

In working toward recovery, those affected by trauma need room to explore their responses to fearful events and to expand their limited emotional arena—time to grieve their losses and express their fears. Denial of such appropriate responses to the upheaval of trauma—often by well-meaning caregivers, family, and friends who advise the sufferer to "get over it and get on with life"—can lead instead to increased social isolation and self-blame.

In working toward recovery, those affected by trauma need time to grieve their losses and express their fears.

The encouragement and participation of supportive others can be essential to a trauma sufferer's successful recovery. For trauma sufferers to reclaim a basic level of trust, it is important that their supporters understand and validate the courage and strength it takes for the survivor to get through the day. Trauma survivors can draw on this newly discovered safety in relationships to develop a greater appreciation of their own worth and competence. With such inspiration, the road to recovery becomes less daunting and the survivor's chance of success greatly improved.

For victims of trauma, the balance of life often swings moment to moment. But through connection and creativity, opportunities abound.

Coming to Terms with Loss

Although we may wish otherwise, endings are inevitable and necessary to allow access to new beginnings. For this very reason, flexibility is essential to survival.

In the aftermath of trauma, however, survivors often become inflexible, fearing more unmanageable change on the horizon. Events related to the trauma seem to keep playing out in unpredictable ways for survivors because trauma memories have never been processed for long-term storage. Those suffering from PTSD have never fully grieved their losses.

For trauma victims, loss takes over their world—especially a loss that is sudden or that has severe, life-changing consequences. The survivor may view every encounter and experience differently, depending on whether it happens before or after the loss.

For trauma victims, loss takes over their world—especially a loss that is sudden or that has severe, life-changing consequences.

My own short-term reference for events that took place before my cancer diagnosis is "BC"—before cancer. For me, BC events have a sepia-toned feel— colored by a nostalgia and innocence that seem sweet but naive in contrast to both the harshly lit experiences of cancer and the bright, but at times tenuous, energy of my present "AC" (after cancer) life. Perhaps the harsh experiences will one day also fall into soft shades of memory; but my perspective will certainly never return to the complacency of the past. The change wrought to my soul by my personal trauma will always frame my present and future—as is likely the case for almost every trauma survivor.

Complex Grief

Even when a loss is intense, time has a calming, distancing influence on the grief that one feels in the aftermath. The death of a beloved but aged grandparent, for example, is felt keenly, but its disruption is typically of limited duration; we go on with our lives. But in the case of an unexpected or unusual loss—the homicide or suicide of a close friend or relative, for example, or an experience of assault—the event may be more than the human mind can effectively process.

The complex grief that survivors experience in such instances is often characterized by obsessive thinking about the loss. Observers may notice that the trauma survivor revisits the same comments—even after the subject of conversation has changed. In addition, the survivor's speech may be pressured and emotions high as the reality of loss returns to his awareness in shock waves of grief.

Until emotional material is processed, it tends to activate an area of the midbrain called the cingulate gyrus. This is the place of obsessive thinking and intense stimulation of ideas. "Why me?" is a frequent refrain, as is "If only this or that had (or hadn't) happened, things would be different."

Like the gyroscope that shares the linguistic root of the term, the cingulate gyrus spins around in a whirl of activity, causing the individual to visit ideas over and over until the ideas can eventually find a place of rest. It is as if the individual needs to continually return to the event to consider its implications in each and every separate area of life. Alternatively, obsessive thoughts or compulsive behaviors will serve to distract and distance them from the intensity of their fear and loss.

> Obsessive thinking is the brain's way of gradually allowing the "new normal" to enter into the individual's concept of future. But it may take a long time to shift old expectations about safety and health, or the availability of a loved one, to new neural structures in the brain that accommodate change. In some cases, professional intervention may be needed to aid in that process.

With opportunity to view past experiences from a new perspective, the trauma survivor's memories of loss can finally reach a point of completion and the emotional overload associated with the overwhelming experience can be reduced to a more manageable burden. Then, a sense of calm can override the agitation of the individual's initial response to loss, and safe, structured relationships can create opportunities for the heart and soul to heal.

Anger and Loss

Anger usually gets a bad rap. Certainly out-of-control anger (rage) is problematic and may have even been a source of early trauma—for example, if an alcoholic parent frequently directed anger toward family members. However, anger's important role in the grieving process has long been recognized.[4]

Anger is more than just acting out frustration. It is a legitimate, critical aspect of moving through trauma recovery. For trauma survivors, arriving at anger and attributing responsibility to the true source rather than engaging in self-blame, are essential elements of recovery.

"Difficult" children and adolescents, for example, are often discovered to be expressing anger at having been mistreated or unsupported in a problem situation. Similarly, patients who fail to cooperate with doctors and nurses in their treatment may be acting on their anger at being saddled with a condition they did not choose and that they feel incapable of managing.

Clearly, anger is closely aligned with fear. By bearing this connection in mind, and avoiding taking the anger personally, a survivor's supporters stand a stronger chance of facilitating a true and lasting recovery.

AVOIDING CAREGIVER BURNOUT

When faced with another person's struggle, especially suffering that has been forced on someone for whom we care deeply, our initial response tends to be one of compassion—with the goal of supporting the loved one's recovery efforts. Following some types of loss, this approach works quite well, allowing the injured party to heal in a supportive environment and gradually reassume the challenges of normal living. In the case of trauma that results in a post-traumatic stress response, however, this approach may fail.

The cycle of intrusion and numbing that is often found among trauma victims is like a broken record: the victim keeps returning to the earlier part of the song (the traumatic injury) rather than playing through to the end (recovery). For this reason, a caregiver's compassionate response can be met with dismal failure. In the worst case, the relationship between survivor and caregiver can be irreparably destroyed. (See appendix B for more on the challenges to supportive relationships.)

To prevent such outcomes and sustain their supporting role, caregivers must be crystal clear about their own boundaries in the care-giving role. Avoiding the controlling influence of a traumatized individual's demanding and withholding behavior pattern is essential. Caregivers who fail in this task may find it necessary to abandon the relationship to survive their own "compassion fatigue."[5]

Caregivers must be crystal clear about their own boundaries in the care-giving role.

Self-awareness can help the caregiver determine the "right" place to set supportive boundaries that can be sustained against a barrage of resistance and attempts at control by the trauma sufferer. Consider how you feel when a telemarketer's phone call interrupts your family dinner or a neighbor's car blocks access to your driveway. If you feel the muscles in your jaw or "gut" tighten in such situations, your body is alerting you to the need to protect your personal resources by saying, "no" or at least, "not right now." The key is developing an awareness of what your bodymind is signaling you in such situations.

By setting appropriate limits and then applying self-awareness skills, caregivers can more effectively manage their support roles with a lowered risk of emotional burnout—for the mutual benefit of both themselves and the trauma survivor.[6]

Notes

1. Bessel A. van der Kolk, Alexander C. McFarlane, and Lars Weisaeth, *Traumatic Stress: The Effects of Overwhelming Experience on Mind, Body, and Society* (New York: Guilford, 1996), 214–41.

2. Erik H. Erikson, *Identity: Youth and Crisis* (New York: Norton, 1968), 247–74.

3. van der Kolk, McFarlane, and Weisaeth, *Traumatic Stress*, 214–41.

4. Dorothy S. Becvar, *In the Presence of Grief: Helping Family Members Resolve Death, Dying and Bereavement Issues* (New York: Guilford, 2001), 24–44.

5. Charles Figley, ed., *Compassion Fatigue: Coping with Secondary Traumatic Stress Disorder in Those Who Treat the Traumatized* (London: Routledge, 1995), 1–20.

6. Laura van Dernoot Lipsky, *Trauma Stewardship: An Everyday Guide to Caring for Yourself While Caring for Others* (San Francisco: Barrett-Koehler, 2009), 41–46.

Acknowledge your fears, but do not cling to them.

three

RECOVERING SELF

Going Public

The change began two weeks after my first chemotherapy treatment, just after the start of the new year. I'd seen increasing amounts of hair in my comb and on my pillow, but nothing had prepared me for the shock of seeing wads of hair in my hand as I stood under the shower. Looking in the mirror confirmed my distress: the woman I saw reminded me of the scrawny zombie in the "Tales from the Crypt" TV horror program.

My main concern was to get rid of the remaining straggles of hair on my head before the kids got home from school. As I sat in the living room trying to take it in, a friend appeared at the door with a "mercy meal," took one look at me, and asked, "Would you like me to get the rest of that off?"

In some ways, it was a relief to have my appearance match my internal state of devastation. Although I'd prepared for the event by purchasing the recommended wig, it made me feel worse instead of better; the wig was a false show, a pretense that everything was OK. So when I was out of the house, I wrapped my head in bright cotton scarves or wore deep-brimmed hats to cover my bare scalp.

*****

Mornings meant having to face myself—groggy, sometimes nauseated, sometimes aching from chemotherapy, and bald. I considered moving the mirror that faced my side of the bed, but that morning glimpse turned out to be the way to find acceptance of my circumstances.

Among my concerns was the reaction that my two-year-old nephew, Zachary, would have on seeing my bald head. But on viewing my head after my scarf had slipped off during one of our afternoon naps, he merely said with a little chuckle, "You look like Paw-Paw," using his name for my bald, bespectacled father.

People commented on the variety of hats I wore—all soft and deep to warm my head—and greeted me with cheering comments. Even my clients were able to see beyond their own pain and look to my changed appearance as a symbol of my engagement in a struggle similar to their own. Suddenly, there was a shift in their remarks during our sessions from "you wouldn't understand" to "you know what it's like." And they were right. I was only beginning to appreciate the day-to-day struggle to cope with profound uncertainty.

In a way, the loss of my hair became my badge of courage, an opportunity to grapple with my changing physical image and with how others responded to the change. I realized that I had to let go of the illusion of control and work at developing faith in my own healing powers.

Visualize what you seek.

The word *recovery* gets a lot of attention these days. In fact, it has the distinction of being considered a movement—a status that shows how many of us feel damaged by the "slings and arrows of outrageous fortune,"[1] whether from the pain and loss of trauma or the seemingly constant struggles of daily living.

But what exactly are we talking about when we say *recovery*? Recover what? Recovery to where? The answer seems to lie in the concept of a return to Self—not the "working model of self" that all of us have developed from our early interactions, but a place of awareness and compassion where we feel in balance and right with the world. That's Self with a capital "S."

If it sounds like the same old New Age language you may have heard many times, too vague and nonspecific to put into action, it isn't. The difference is found in its resonance with who you are—*wherever you are in the course of your life*. This is recovery, after all, which implies that you aren't where you want to be in some essential way.

Before you read on, stop for a moment to think of a best time in your life. If you look back over your life story for moments, however brief, of contentment and rightness with the world, what do they include? Breathe in and out as you look at the elements of that time. Is there someone with you? What are you communicating and experiencing in that moment?

It is certain that the moment that you accessed wasn't a time of criticism and stress, but a moment of clarity and acceptance. *How good that feels!*

The most important element of recovery is a felt truth within the Self. If we depend only on "the kindness of strangers"—or even the support of those closest to us—to fill our need for unconditional acceptance, we'll come up short. The reality is, it would be *impossible* for any other person to be consistently in tune with our emotional need for acceptance, no matter how much the person cares about us. Accessing and accepting our Self is an energizing, healing opportunity. The only way to extend this sense of Self-energy is to hold and support it from within.

The most important element of recovery is a felt truth within the Self.

The place where recovery begins and expands is in the calm quiet of your own mind, body, and heart. If you depend solely on how others respond to you, they may distract you from your recovery through their own challenges or a limited sense of their own worth. But when you *mindfully* engage with Self-energy in interpersonal or intrapersonal (internally directed) connections, wonderful things can happen.

INTERNAL FAMILY SYSTEMS THEORY

Drawn from professional experience working with survivors of developmental trauma, Internal Family Systems (IFS) therapy directs therapists not to try to "fix" what's "wrong" with a trauma victim, but instead to engage their own *Self-energy* to help the survivor achieve *Self-leadership*.[2] A "healing space" emerges naturally when judgmental thoughts are recognized and revised to a more compassionate form of awareness, gradually embracing the knowledge that everyone has worth.

In applying IFS theory, the therapist assists the trauma survivor to revisit and reshape attachment structures from within. Opportunities for healing, acceptance, and release that arise during the course of the therapy eventually shift the survivor's negative meanings to a stronger, more-balanced awareness and "Self-led" perspective. Through this process, the survivor comes to see parents and other attachment figures in all their flawed reality—and perhaps even eventually to forgive them for those flaws—as judgments and burdens are surrendered to access a more balanced Self-concept.

Among the various approaches to the treatment of trauma, IFS is unique in its focus on internal "Parts." In the IFS model, Parts that have struggled to manage and protect the vulnerable child from distorted attachment experiences are recognized for their caring efforts. Other Parts responsible for damaging behaviors, such as addictions and other compulsive activities, are seen for their protective intent as well, and are invited to participate in opportunities to revise such self-harming approaches in favor of more productive forms of coping.

Ultimately, the emotionally vulnerable child within the trauma sufferer is reengaged, and the confusion of maltreatment, with its inherently distorted meanings, can be resolved. Such deeply integrative work leads naturally to the victim's best Self in internal and external relationships. Through such efforts, the survivor returns to the world with a restored sense of Self-worth.

Access to previously blocked energy is a product of recovery. In releasing the burdens of misunderstanding and emotional pain, we find new resources. Through Self-leadership, opportunities for connection internally and in relationships with others arise, as well as improved physical abilities, sleep patterns, and mood. (Some ways to access these changes are explored in the next part of this book.)

THE TRAUMATIZED BRAIN

Researchers in psychology and neurobiology emphasize the impact of early relationships on brain development.[3] Negative experiences can take (potentially) permanent residence in our nervous systems, effectively blocking us from access to tools for self-regulation and coping that might otherwise be available.

Picture a deep scratch across the face of a compact disc or vinyl long-play record that alters the pattern of the imprinted vibrations that create a song. The deep cut will displace the tracking device to a different groove in the soundtrack of our past, disorienting us by skipping to the wrong place and essentially disrupting the flow of our life music. At the same time, the skip highlights the loss of a favorite tune. If we perceive this loss as threatening, we tend to avoid getting anywhere near chaotic noise, leaving us scrambling to change the record, or distract ourselves from the trauma.

Therapists and others in shared recovery journeys can effectively attend to, and foster changes in, brain patterns that were forged by trauma. The therapist or other relationship partner can serve the role of disc jockey, halting the interminable broken record by smoothing over the disconnect and helping the victim put it away in a safe place. Simultaneously, the victim and therapist can work in partnership to develop new tracks in the "life recording" that emphasize competence and self-worth through attention to the "now" instead of the "then."

In demonstrating caring interest in their recovery partner's perspective, supporters can actually modify perceptual patterns in the traumatized individual, creating new connections and offering reparative experiences as the trauma loosens its hold on the survivor's nervous system.

Mind and Body Recovery

Early visual and auditory stimulation can hardwire messages from responsive, or neglectful, primary caregivers.[4] A smiling face, engaged expression, clear focus and calming voice are the basis for the fundamental sense of self-in-the-world of a newborn infant. These data are stored deep in the limbic system, the place where self-calming mechanisms are available. Internalization of that regulatory model is the bottom line of mental health and relationship management—or of their opposite, depending on what was modeled.

Research findings reinforce the critical role of attachment on the long-term, self-regulatory capacities of emotional management. Evidence supporting the bio-psycho-social implications of trauma includes the realm of early neural programming (brain connections) and the development of new options for repair within the context of later healing relationships. Because of these adaptive functions, old neural connections can be reviewed and updated with new information, even into later life.

Attachment-based processes are most flexible and open to new information during infancy, but "neuroplasticity"—the nervous system's ability to be revised or added to—is available throughout our lives. Change can occur most effectively through the healing experience of calm, focused interaction with caring others.

The role of the body in psychotherapy has been long recognized but not always effectively used to help in trauma victims' healing process. Recently, attention to physical responses and bodily representations of stored traumatic memories have moved to center stage in the treatment milieu, with positive results for those in recovery.

Blocked or incomplete action is a source of many of the symptoms of trauma in individuals. But activities that allow the victim to bypass these self-protective blocks can be very effective in strengthening and supporting healthy functioning and helping the survivor maintain resiliency in the face of life's many challenges. Healthy forms of movement, for example, yoga and dance, can be incorporated into the recovery process, as can artistic representations of internal struggle and release.

In addition, self-care practices related to the management of sleep and nutrition can help keep the body in a healthy state, supporting therapeutic efforts to guide the victim toward a positive future based on respect for the Self and grounded in respectful relationships.

Self-care practices can help keep the body in a healthy state, supporting therapeutic efforts.

Through active engagement with the bodymind to access, acknowledge, and release stored trauma responses, we can open to new opportunities for healing. Recovery demands awareness and willingness to know the effects of traumatic loss, along with attention to the relative safety of the present.

Opportunities for emotional and physical release abound when the trauma response is explored and expressed, allowing us to reset the nervous system and engage with the compassionate and competent present-moment energy of Self.

Notes

1. William Shakespeare, *The Complete Works of William Shakespeare*, vol. 3, ed. David Bevington (New York: Bantam, 1988), 59.

2. Richard C. Schwartz, *Internal Family Systems Therapy* (New York: Guilford, 1995), 27–57.

3. Diana Foshe, Daniel J. Siegel, and Marion F. Solomon, eds., *The Healing Power of Emotion: Affective Neuroscience and Clinical Practice* (New York: Norton, 2009).

4. Stephen Porges, *The Polyvagal Theory: The Neurophysiological Foundation of Emotions, Attachment, Communication and Self-Regulation* (New York: Norton, 2011), 52–61.

THE SECOND PART

GOING WITH FLOWING

This second part of the book explores the question at the heart of this work: How does healing happen? In this part, I introduce an acronym—FLOWING—to describe a powerful, holistic, Self-led process that can guide trauma survivors in recovery. The strength and substance of the FLOWING model is its continuous nature and the opportunity for the trauma survivor to engage the process at any point, through a variety of approaches.

Each of the seven letters of FLOWING stands for a word that can offer guidance along the path of recovery. The first four letters of the acronym (FLOW) are presented in this second part of the book; the remaining letters (ING) are discussed in the third part.

Chapter four—focusing on the F in FLOWING—describes the importance of bodymind attention to how we *feel* as the way to *find* our present-moment experience. By connecting with our physical and emotional senses, each of us can engage with our unique experience of loss and with the meaning we infer from that experience.

In chapter five, the focus turns to the second letter of FLOWING, L, which stands for *listen*. Through active *listening*, we can engage with internally held meanings that, once acknowledged, can promote recovery. Mindfulness-based practices offer many opportunities for attuned *listening*.

Chapter six—focusing on O, the third letter of FLOWING—discusses the importance of an *open* heart, a heart without judgment or prejudice. By adopting an attitude of acceptance of whatever arises, we are *open* to accessing elements of our experience that might otherwise be shrouded in shame. The ancient concept of chakras offers guidance in bringing our body energies into the recovery process.

The fourth letter of FLOWING, W, discussed in chapter seven, points to the importance of bearing *witness* to what we have learned about ourselves in early relationships. To change negative attachment-based patterns, we must actively represent the unmet needs of our internal "Parts" that have been wronged. Body-based therapies can help us move beyond basic mindfulness practices to *witness* and heal both our bodymind and our relationships.

Seek your own truth.

four

FEEL: FINDING FLOWING

Spirit Guide: The Hawk

After receiving my cancer diagnosis, I quickly realized that I was in dire need of new resources to help me cope with the anxiety I was experiencing. I had a friend who had recently trained in hypnotherapy techniques, and I called to ask for her help.

When Denise arrived at my home, I immediately felt calmer. She first listened to my two central fears: burdening my family and counteracting my healing efforts with overwhelming anxiety. Then, coaching me through focused breathing and progressive relaxation, Denise asked me to develop a mantra, a phrase or sound that would bring me comfort and concentrate my internal resources.

As Denise led me through a series of visualizations of my own healing resources, she instructed me to respectfully request an internal sign to guide my healing. To my surprise—since I'd never had much luck with guided imagery efforts—I caught in my mind's eye a glimpse of something that appeared to be the tip of a hawk's wing. I had a sense of being carried and protected, and I decided to embrace the hawk as my healing guide.

Regularly practicing the breathing and guided imagery in the days and weeks that followed helped calm my fears and lessened the pain and nausea that I experienced from my surgeries and subsequent chemotherapy. My surgeons commented on my limited use of pain medications and my rapid healing, which I took as proof of the effectiveness of these efforts.

My relaxation sessions settled into a rhythm of breath and mental repetition of words expressing my hope for health and safety, followed by slipping into a sense of flying on the shoulders of the red-tailed hawk, my spirit guide. Impressions of soaring over low rolling hills above glimmering trails of water led me to wordless understanding of their meaning: my hawk guide was searching for anything that was out of place to eliminate like vermin—much as the chemotherapy was eliminating any rogue cancer cells that might compromise my recovery.

These sessions frequently left me with brief glimpses of powerful images, like snapshots of healing, which I later represented in my artist journal using colored pencils. I captured these scenes on paper, allowing me to revisit them later to consider their full meaning.

* * * * *

In the months that followed, chemotherapy left me drained and depressed, and my former identity as competent and in control changed forever. At the halfway point in my chemo treatments, my doctors shifted me to a different poison to further promote the destruction of my cancer. But with my hair long gone, my eyebrows and lashes quickly disappearing, painful sores in my mouth, and my body bloated from steroids, I was physically and emotionally exhausted. I began to think I might never make it through the chemo, much less the radiation treatments to follow.

To distract and support me, my friend Jenny invited me to visit the mountain lodge in Arizona where we'd spent time during high school. The promise that my dear friend would care for me and offer me a brief escape from my world of discomfort and fear was enough to get me on a plane. Along with another friend, Vicky, we set off for the White Mountains.

On our second full day, Jenny proposed a short hike along a trail at the top of the mountain. I doubted my endurance, but we agreed that the hike could end at any time I felt the need. The trail passed through a section of new-growth aspen trees, interspersed with blackened stumps from hardwoods that had burned in a forest fire decades earlier. The air was clear and the sounds of the forest were musical, but I soon began to run out of steam in the high altitude. Jenny was anxious to go farther, to access a view she wanted us to share, so she continued along the trail while Vicky and I waited in a quiet glen.

I took the opportunity to meditate to try to gather more strength for the next leg of the hike. Soon, I found myself immersed in images of my hawk guide soaring just above the tree line. The soft breeze and the call of birds, along with the effects of altitude and tired muscles, led to the clearest imagery I'd ever experienced, and the result was breathtaking in its power. When I opened my eyes sometime later, Vicky sat with me and listened to my story of the healing images.

When Jenny returned from her explorations, she told us that the spot she wanted us to see was an easy ten-minute hike. Explaining her longer-than-expected delay, she said, "There was a beautiful red-tailed hawk circling around while I sat there; it was so lovely, I couldn't bring myself to leave."

Vicky looked at me and gasped, "It was you!" My hawk guide energy had seemingly attracted, or perhaps manifested as, a physical representation of itself.

We completed the hike to a view that was well worth the effort. I was buoyed by the beautiful scene, the powerful experience of meditation, and the manifestation of my experience—all shared with two close friends. Later, I recorded the images of the view and of the burned stumps in the forest surrounded by new growth.

* * * * *

In subsequent months, I realized that creating and expressing those images of renewal at work in the world of nature had led me to revise my attitude and expectations about the radiation treatments. Through connection with my internal resources and engagement with the natural world, I found healing energy where I had feared no more was available.

In a process that had taken place quite unconsciously, my fears of burning loss had been replaced with images of new and healthy blossoming spirit. I recorded those images and events as colorful representations of my internal processes, to hold onto their power in visual and expressive form. Those experiences and images went far toward reinforcing the strength of my early healing efforts and my resolve to push through the dark times of cancer—and even to perhaps offer new light to others on their own recovery journeys.

Keep your goals in sight, and put one foot in front of the other.

The way to truly know ourselves is to be attentive to how we *feel*—to engage with and experience our emotions. But today's get-over-it approach to life, with its quick-fix remedies, often discounts the internally focused attention that is the basis for recovery. My clients who have experienced great loss typically focus desperately on not *feeling*, not knowing. But because trauma is essentially a collection of unintegrated experiences, it can be resolved only through emotional awareness.

EMOTIONS AND HEALING

For trauma survivors, attention to emotional responses—especially as they relate to significant relationships in repeating patterns or themes—is the key to accessing the FLOWING energies of Self. True Self-energy is a state of calm awareness. Recovery efforts therefore must include the gradual reworking of blocked or distorted emotions. Then, through a physiological process of "neural rewiring," connections in the brain are actually modified, and interpersonal and intrapersonal connections improved, with lasting effects. In other words, we must *feel* to *heal*.

What Are Emotions?

Emotions are collections of *felt* meaning with accompanying physiological cues that activate and shape our life experiences. Emotions tend to form around feelings that emerge from our primary attachment relationships early in life, creating positive self-images and expectations, or negative interpretations of experiences. From these expectations and interpretations, we develop an image of self that is dominated by themes of either acceptance or defense. If we defend against all *feelings* to avoid the negative ones, we tend to miss out on important opportunities for positive emotions, draining life experiences of their color and richness.

As these themes are further reinforced by our relationships and experiences across the lifespan, they constantly color the lens through which we view the world—and even the energy that we attract. Our emotional receptors cause us to interpret interpersonal cues through the lens of our default setting, resulting in positive or defensive expectations. Just as a person bitten by dog might avoid contact with dogs in the future, so is our future behavior guided by our past experience.

Being out of touch with our emotions can have serious implications for our relationships and our health. Among people who are not closely attuned to their emotions, harmful physical changes can occur quite subtly. Unexpressed emotions can eventually build up to a point of disrupting our movement through life. For example, an assault survivor might become so fearful that they avoid leaving the house, making it impossible to participate in, benefit from, and enjoy healthy social relationships.

Unexpressed emotions can build up to a point of disrupting our movement through life.

Some, including victims of trauma, may suppress or deny "negative" *feelings*, pushing them down with food, a focus on perfectionism, or other self-destructive activities. But the energy expended on restricting emotional expression takes a toll, creating blocked internal and relational communication. These areas of "stuckness" gain expression in the form of illness, autoimmune disorders, anxiety, and depression. Try as we might to hide out from painful or frightening emotions, they find us.

Emotional receptors draw on what they need in an instinctual quest for balance. This is certainly true of the biologically driven emotional functioning inherent in, and essential to, human existence. Our bioengineered, metaphysical makeup adapts for survival of the species with expectations and coping skills structured around the central task of self-preservation.

Coping and protecting "Parts" evolve in each of us to negotiate the ins and outs of daily life. Parts are "triggered" to play their role by the release of neurochemicals that classify and respond to the emerging social environment in milliseconds, long before any conscious evaluation of the interaction begins. Their mission: to protect and ensure the survival of the Self.

Accessing and Expressing Emotions

Accessing our emotions can be a complex undertaking. Those who experience trauma at a very young age, for example, often develop a "don't ask, don't tell" policy when it comes to expressing their emotions. But with the right tools and guidance, and commitment to the process, even individuals suffering from developmental damage can gain access to their emotions and actively participate in change. Body-awareness practices promote a sense of calm; and in a calm environment, wellness can be accessed through creative expression and self-care. From there, we can *feel* our way into FLOWING, a step-by-step process of recovery.

Ancient traditions have long taught that accessing one's inner world can be a tool for change on personal and global levels, and Western cultures are rediscovering Buddhist and Hindu meditation practices. These traditional practices, which actually change the brain through neuroplasticity, today are at the forefront of the practice of psychotherapy.[1] But a degree in neuroscience isn't necessary to receive the benefit of this marriage of ancient practice and leading-edge intervention. With some knowledge and dedication, anyone can gain the healing benefits of self-awareness.

SELF-EXPRESSION AND PERSONAL DEVELOPMENT

The opposite of creativity is stagnation—a "stuck" position in which many victims of trauma and loss find themselves. The terror of returning to a position of vulnerability and pain is sometimes paralyzing for a trauma victim: any change is perceived as risk, so the individual may stop moving altogether.

But this protective response ultimately limits the trauma victim's options for recovery, creating a self-fulfilling prophesy of the hopeless life. The most successful options for recovery from traumatic loss contain elements of creative expression—virtual opportunities for rebirth beyond the temporary "death" of stagnated development.

The most successful options for recovery from traumatic loss contain elements of creative expression.

Much of the paralysis of trauma has to do with its unprocessed state in primal areas of the human brain. Triggers that bear some reminder of the original trauma event (or events) can be so overwhelming that the individual has no capacity to override them. Asked to revisit the experience of trauma—even in the process of trying to achieve recovery—a victim is likely to feel terrified. Because these affective reminders emerge as pure feeling, without rhyme or reason, they are often more accessible through indirect or expressive means.

Art and movement practices are highly effective in releasing us from the rigid, fearful position of trauma victim, allowing us to externalize meanings and represent them in symbolic form. Then, once a reasonable amount of the trauma response has been accessed and expressed, it becomes more possible to try to engage compassionately with hurt within the Self-system and to approach healing undeterred by overriding emotional burdens.

Art and movement practices are effective in releasing us from the rigid, fearful position of trauma victim.

Therapeutic Self-Expression

Expressive therapies—painting a picture, sketching an image of a desired future, journaling about fears, engaging in movement such as dance or exercise, and myriad other expressions of meaning—offer trauma victims release in ways that bypass direct confrontation with the stark realities of hurt and loss. Through such therapies, unconscious or preconscious material can be brought gently to the trauma victim's awareness.

If the choice of expression is in the form of writing or drawing, the effort can be put away for later consideration in a safe, therapeutic environment. Or the expressive work might be created only to be destroyed, in a literal process of catharsis providing relief to the victim.

Expression can also take place in more directed ways, through movement, sculpture, or other physical actions. Sharing or creating these expressive pieces in the presence of a trained therapist provides the safety that the victim needs; the therapist can take the observer role while helping the victim recognize and work with metaphors that imbue the process.

One need not create something qualifying as "art" to benefit from investing in such a personal process. Options for expression are as limitless as paralyzed emotional processes are limiting. The very act of expression is a means of creating a new reality: survival in action. Each creative effort brings the trauma victim that much closer to the life that he or she envisions and deserves to live fully.

The very act of expression is
a means of creating a new reality:
survival in action.

Underlying Meanings

The use of symbolic representation in defining experience dates to the earliest days of human existence. Cave paintings, hieroglyphs, petroglyphs, and cuneiform are all examples of early humans' efforts to express their life experiences using symbols.

To effectively represent a thought or *feeling* in language or imagery, we must first take a step back and compare and contrast our internally felt state with related objects or actions. Carl Jung highlighted the concept of the "collective unconscious," a sort of underground stream of meanings that all humans instinctively access to inform their understandings and responses.[2] This shared mental "stream" flows through common elements of human experience in larger-than-life symbolic forms called archetypes.

Archetypes are shared expressions of meaning, wherein common emotional threads weave universal experiences together across cultures. Understanding our own sense of meaning will help us to hold and express empathy for others who are in the midst of their own losses.

Archetypes offer powerful symbolic models for self-awareness and recovery. The meanings that these archetypes carry establish universal expectations that are "hard wired" in our brains. This explains why we recognize that something is "not right" if we're treated unfairly by those in a care-giving role—even if that has been our only experience of "care". Highlighting what "should be" in contrast with "what is" archetypes can provide models for self-awareness, effectively allowing us to *feel* our way to greater clarification of internally experienced meanings.

To fully embrace the *feeling* aspect of FLOWING, we must immerse ourselves in the *meanings* behind our emotions. By taking an image of loss from our mind's eye and then expressing and transforming it in an experiential way, we can create new neural pathways and uncover hidden meanings that inspire change.

Jungian authors such as Jean Shinoda Bolen,[3] Jean Houston,[4] and Clarissa Pinkola Estes[5] write about transformative thinking: discovering purpose beneath pain and confusion. Each uses myth, fable, or other "universal" story lines to bring individual loss into the realm of change and growth. Other artists and storytellers tap into the collective meanings of archetypal images to speak a truth that may be recognizable by many: the lyric of a Joni Mitchell song, for example, or the artistry of Van Gogh's unforgettable "A Starry Night." Shared meanings offer release and a sense that we are not alone in our struggle.

* * * * *

Emotional awareness is the basis for intimacy in relationships. Using the language of imagery, we are recognized by others. Being "seen" for who we are provides opportunities to build trust and access healing. Whether in relationship to others or to an emerging sense of Self, connecting with and expressing our emotions is essential for FLOWING into recovery.

Notes

1. Daniel J. Siegel, *The Mindful Brain: Reflection and Attunement in the Cultivation of Well-Being* (New York: Norton, 2007), 209–27.

2. Carl G. Jung, *Collected Works of C. G. Jung*, trans. R. F. C. Hull (Princeton, NJ: Princeton University Press, 1972).

3. Jean Shinoda Bolen, MD, *Goddesses in Everywoman: Powerful Archetypes in Women's Lives* (New York: Harper & Row, 1994).

4. Jean Houston, *A Mythic Life: Learning to Live Our Greater Story* (New York: Harper Collins, 1996), 85–110.

5. Clarissa Pinkola Estes, *Women Who Run With the Wolves: Myths and Stories of the Wild Woman Archetype* (New York: Random House, 1992).

A change of perspective can help you appreciate the big picture in life.

five

LISTEN: FLOWING PRESENCE

Snake That Bit Me

A few weeks after my final radiation treatment, the phone rang. The call was an invitation for me to sing at an event to raise awareness and funding for breast cancer research. The song, as yet unwritten, was to be a celebration of life. Would my husband, the songwriter, like to offer an entry?

The call over, the proposed song title rang in my ears as I put words to paper: "Two Thousand Reasons to Celebrate." The title—a nod to the fast-approaching millennium—would be an anthem of hope for a cure so others might escape what I'd endured. The lyrics spilled from my mind like pearls, with rhymes marking the many tiers of my survival-shaped necklace. Less than two months later, we recorded that heartfelt song, with instrumentation and harmony provided by my husband and my musical siblings.

A group of entertainers who had volunteered to perform met for a pre-event celebration and the song's unveiling. A thrill ran up my spine when one of the performers turned to me and said, "Have you heard the song? It's wonderful!" Here I was, surrounded by local musicians whose names and sounds I'd known for years. As they sang along with the recording, rock-star images from my adolescent fantasies swirled around me in four/four time. How had such a dark, painful year suddenly turned into my dream come true?

Even as I gloried in the sudden sense of celebrity, the nightmare of diagnosis and treatments briefly fading from my mind, a nagging internal voice warned me not to let it "go to my head," intruding on my wish to enjoy the triumph of the moment.

Events took a dramatic turn when after all the others had left, a barefoot walk across the patio flagstones drew my attention to what felt like a dry leaf curled around the middle toe of my left foot. Looking down, I discovered a long, skinny appendage attached—a garden snake of a size I'd never before encountered.

Squeals and curses emerged from me, like a zealot speaking in tongues, as I hopped on one foot and kicked with the other. My husband had the foresight to follow the terrified critter long enough to identify its status as nonvenomous. Further confirmation was provided by the hostess's hasty call to her snake-savvy brother, who reassured that the presence of four punctures (turned to slits by my vigorous kicking response) rather than two ensured that the bite was harmless.

During the next few weeks, I described my remarkable rise and fall to friends and family with a smile, but the ominous biblical overtones of this snake-in-my-garden-of-Eden evening nagged on. One conversation with a journalist who would MC the upcoming event—a breast-cancer survivor herself—prompted her enlightening comment: "You know, in many cultures the snake is considered a sign of new life."

My sense of relief from her comment was immense. Her description of her post-cancer experiences of powerful, symbolic "coincidence" expanded my awareness of the synchronicity that exists throughout our daily lives—if we only pay attention.

By the night of the big event, I was able to celebrate with an open heart and full participation in the joy of the experience. An audience of nine hundred supporters must have felt the same emotions as they stood and clapped along with our song of hope for a cancer-free future.

2000 Reasons to Celebrate

A bolt out of the blue, a wakeup call that's true,
It shakes you to your very foundation.
It's time to think it through, count the blessings offered you,
Start singing out the sudden realization.

There are two thousand reasons to celebrate,
A lot of living left to do.
Two thousand reasons to celebrate
The gifts of life that have been given you.

A tiny infant's cry, an aging grandpa's sigh,
The music of the people on the street,
A hand that you can hold that keeps you from the cold,
Those little things that make a life complete.

So we climb those endless hills, take the needles and the pills,
Doing everything we can to make it right,
Looking forward to the day when our fears will go away
And our sisters will no longer have to fight.

There are two thousand reasons to celebrate,
A lot of living left to do.
Two thousand reasons to celebrate
The gifts of life that have been given you.

Listen to the song of your heart.

The second letter of the FLOWING acronym, L, stands for *listen*. Taking time to *listen* to our *felt* experience allows us to resolve issues that may block access to improved quality of life.

Listening to our deeply held belief systems is best accomplished through the inward-turning practice of mindfulness—the non-judgmental, compassionate awareness of internal and external present-moment experience. Before Western culture embraced mindfulness as a tool for well-being, hermits and monks practiced mindfulness meditation for centuries. The achievement of exquisite moments of glimpsed enlightenment requires compassion and internal loving kindness, permitting us to move toward a higher level of Self-energy. From that position, healing is a natural outcome.

MINDFULNESS PRACTICE

Calm Self-awareness that brings clarity, understanding, and acceptance is a state that many ascribe to. But how can we engage in effective mindfulness practice?

Instead of focusing on things that are over and done and can't be changed—or things that could be problems if they arose in the future—we can, through mindfulness, be in the moment, in *the now*. Living in the present moment is far more promising and meaningful than living in a world of memory, illusion, or fearful conjecture. Of course, there will be times when we need to plan ahead or when we "walk down memory lane." But it is empowering to actively choose to reflect at those moments—rather than to passively allow past events or fears of the future to fill our minds and define our place in the world.

Compassion is the key element in any mindfulness practice. *Listening* to our inner world compassionately and without judgment leads to a healthy emotional and physical life—a balanced life.

Practicing mindfulness requires attention to our internal states of being: emotion, sensation, and energy. *Listening* mindfully also requires external awareness: our sense of place in relationship to others and to the world around. When we practice mindfulness, the body is our temple, and our relationship with the natural world is the shrine.

When we practice mindfulness,
the body is our temple,
and our relationship with
the natural world is the shrine.

Mindfulness and Breathing

The road to a mindful state is through breathing. By focusing on the intricacies of taking in and then releasing our breath, we can't help but be in the present moment.[1] Subtleties of movement, sensation, temperature, circulation of blood, and the functioning of internal organs all are supported by breath. A focus on the flow of our breathing allows our thoughts and images to flow as well. When such "unspoken communications" are the objects of our *listening*, we gain an opportunity to heal and grow in meaningful ways.

The mind is not merely a function of the brain. It's an embodied system of physical and emotional elements working together to frame our experience of life. If we attend only to the intellectual, the emotional elements of the mind stagnate; by contrast, if we're preoccupied by thoughts, the body suffers from lack of expression. Our efforts at recovery and forward momentum need to be engaged, and *listened to* at multiple levels of mindful activity. Connection with the breath immediately slows the heartbeat and optimizes oxygen levels throughout the body, calming the nervous system and improving organ functioning. The resulting calm of inhalation is literally "inspiring" in its contribution to awareness and wellness.

Psychotherapy and Mindfulness

Psychotherapy relies on "efficacy-based" interventions for improved functioning. With the advent of new technologies for scanning brain activity, more direct evidence of neurobiological change is available. It has become clear that with the incorporation of mindfulness in psychotherapy, effective, balanced recovery outcomes are possible. Through an awareness of the protective roadblocks that arise in a therapeutic setting, mindfulness makes it possible for trauma victims to *listen* to and correct distorted messages.

> Developmental relationships, including those formed during therapy, are essentially connections between the right brains of those participating in shared interactions.[2] Reflections of meaning between relationship partners (parent-child, adult-other, client-therapist) shape our sense of self through brain-to-brain transmissions, for good or ill. Attuned interactions contribute to calming and healing the nervous system in survivors of trauma.

Rather than "plug in" an intervention—for example, "Take two pills, and call me in the morning"—the therapist who helps a trauma victim discover and practice mindfulness gently guides the individual to access internal processes and implied meanings, creating opportunities for engaging their innate capacity for recovery. Mindful recovery occurs when we clear away problematic meanings and find our natural state of goodness and health.

Mindful recovery occurs when we clear away problematic meanings and find our natural state of goodness and health.

Many Roads to Mindfulness

The options for accessing mindfulness are as many and varied as are the individuals who seek to open up to such growth-enhancing experiences. Grouping mindfulness practices into four broad categories offers a view of the breadth of choices.

- **Meditation**—Practiced since ancient times, attention to one's experience of internally directed consciousness has long been considered a primary path to enlightenment. Meditative practices continue be a cornerstone of many spiritual traditions—whether sound driven (chanting, *listening* to chimes) or silent contemplation; emptying the mind or filling it with a single-minded focus; or ongoing nonattached awareness of moment-by-moment experiencing. Secular meditation practices are on the rise in Western societies.
- **Yoga and body therapies**—Since body and mind are one interconnected entity, any process that allows for nonjudgmental awareness of one's internal and

external state is by definition a mindful state. With such attention, almost any focused activity—a sensory activity (*listening* to birdsong or music, seeing a flower's petals or smelling its essence, tasting a favorite food, *feeling* the healing touch of massage, or other energy work) or engaging our bodies in flowing movement (yoga, dance, tai-chi)—can result in a sense of present-moment calm. Body-awareness experiences, a cornerstone of trauma release therapy, may be essential to fully accessing stored distortions as well as developing trust in our own resources.

- **Artistic expression**—Symbols speak volumes. The adage, "A picture is worth a thousand words" is true not only for representative artworks but perhaps even more so for the abstract and personal expression of inner conflicts and celebrations of Self. Practical arts like weaving and textile works can offer solace in their very rhythm and flow at a level of unconscious expression, opening the Self to unbiased creativity and recognition of meaning.
- **Mindfulness-based therapies**—Mindfulness is an element of many therapeutic models and practices, used to promote relaxation and to help clients calm. Internal Family Systems (IFS) therapy is a form of psychotherapy that uses mindful attention to access healing. IFS theory offers an open-ended structure for accessing internal guidance and for working supportively with protective "Parts" of the Self-system instead of judging them to be negative influences. In IFS, every Part is recognized for its coping function, despite having become less effective over the long term. Internal and external compassion offer a pathway to change

> through Self-awareness and Self-leadership. How much more wise and safe an option is this than pharmacologically blocked awareness or a cognitively enforced version of someone else's "truth"?

Alone or in combination, these therapeutic practices can enhance a trauma survivor's recovery process in ways unique to their own unfolding journey. Whether achieved with the guidance of a licensed healing professional or through independent efforts, it is only through *listening* to our own internal voice that we can *open* to new understanding of our personal path through healing.

Time, Trauma, and Mindfulness

Spiritual teacher Eckhart Tolle[3] has written powerfully and clearly about the role of time in spiritual practice. He makes the case that we should not allow time, with its deceptive constraints of past and future, to dominate our perspective of life:

> What you think of as the past is a memory trace, stored in the mind, of a former Now. When you remember the past you reactivate a memory trace—and you do so now. The future is an imagined Now, a projection of the mind. When the future comes, it comes as the Now. When you think about the future, you do it now. Past and future obviously have no reality of their own.[4]

In other words, what is happening *this moment* is the only reality; all else is mere mental activity. In the life of a trauma survivor, however, past experience has a tenacious hold, so strong that, for the survivor, it seems nearly impossible to even attend to the idea of *Now*. Trauma's unprocessed form keeps it raw and thus held by the survivor's mind as an active, present-moment experience. For this reason, the efforts of friends and loved ones to encourage the survivor's attention to the present moment can be futile if the traumatized individual fears being immediately swamped by terror and pain.

At the heart of the survivor's difficulty and pain is the fact that the brain holds unprocessed experiences, thoughts, and feelings in a completely different location from where processed memories are stored. So for the traumatized survivor, the practice of attending mindfully to present-moment internal and external experience becomes a confusing, often shame-inducing effort.

Rather than a just-do-it approach, mindful awareness requires gradual establishment of a sense of Self in the present moment. Working compassionately with Parts that hold traumatic or otherwise painful messages can allow us to actively process the distorted information without being flooded by remembered pain. At the level of the nervous system, an unblocking takes place, offering space for new experiences to be engaged and considered for their corrective meanings.

From this point, the conceptual material is processed into more memory-based expression and storage, effectively minimizing or eliminating outdated autonomic response patterns of severe reactivity. The outcome of all this activity is *integration* of the trauma into memory, allowing the survivor to grieve losses and begin to heal. (See chapter seven for more about *integration.*)

SELF-LEADERSHIP

The Self-leadership perspective of Internal Family Systems (IFS) theory is an effective approach to the *integrative* trauma processing described above. This model contains elements that guide trauma processing without further disrupting the survivor's life.

There is no need for training in brain chemistry or neural processing to participate effectively in this therapy. But it is useful to know that IFS combines elements of mindful awareness and body work to help the survivor release the emotional burdens of trauma.

Internally directed explorations of meaningful events and images offer opportunities to *listen* to and resolve past hurts, while *opening* up space for healing energies throughout the mind and body. These energies affect physical (immune system, biochemical processes), emotional (mental health, relationships), and ultimately spiritual (existential, theological, universal) growth— all innately interconnected elements.

Although IFS is not the only effective option, its strength is in its relationship focus. That focus is applied not only to external relationships but, more important for recovery from trauma, to internal systemic elements. This network of Parts protects the survivor and offers time and space to recover from traumatic events. Because these stored trauma burdens may later become "radioactive," emitting signals and triggering overblown reactions to general life experiences, they must be addressed, and emotional blocks released, to allow for a greater range of options for coping with life challenges as they arise. Once again, the mind, body, and Self-in-relationship represent their collective and inseparable nature.

In the weeks following the loss of my mother, I had a dream of startling clarity. My dream featured our newly constructed house addition and my confusion about its purpose, now that my mother would not live there. Instead of modern construction, it took on the proportions and form of a Roman amphitheater. Paths wound around and under stone archways, and people wandered about. The building foreman, who pointed out details in the carved doors to the outdoor stage, was my mentor in my upcoming IFS training (Dick Schwartz). The images in this dream were vivid, and I woke wondering at the intensity of feeling and clarity it had evoked.

Weeks later, the training began. After some initial presentations and demonstrations, the participants separated to work in small groups. When, as a designated "client," I spoke about distraction from Parts, fearing disapproval of such "self-indulgent" explorations, a suggestion was made to move them to an "auditorium" where they could watch the action without disrupting. In my internal view, the auditorium shifted quickly to the amphitheater in my dream.

In subsequent IFS training, my meditations featured that space as a center of activity—a place where Parts and Self could meet, from which pathways led to an expanding internal landscape. As the training weekends progressed, the landscape extended to a distant snow-capped peak touched by radiant sunlight. I understood it to be a symbol of enlightenment and Self-actualization, distant but attainable with consistent effort.

These far reaches connect to the amphitheater via arid, rocky foothills—hard-to-cross terrain. These boulder-strewn, gritty areas are daunting, full of bad habits and resentments, losses and struggles to keep moving; but the obstructions are easier to face for knowing that places of comfort and unfolding Self-awareness lie just beyond the horizon.

The complexities of this inner landscape aside, its purpose is clear. This is the place to meet and communicate with Parts—those elements of Self-energy that hold emotional connections, body awareness, and meaning-making and coping structures: our way of being in the world. In the landscape of Self, we can interact with these Parts, nurturing awareness of their influence on our perceptions and choices. In doing so, we can promote movement of those energies that may have been blocked, contributing to emotional and physical unease and illness. The content of such blocks is as unique as the life experiences, personality factors, and attachment qualities of every individual, yet the process of allowing information to flow across mind/body/spirit systems is essential to health in the entire spectrum of Self.[5]

The providential timing of my IFS training allowed me to discover and explore these aspects of Self in a supportive, consistent group environment, where members shared their own internal explorations, vulnerabilities, and frustrations. The fit between the IFS model and recent "discoveries" of mindfulness as effective in facilitating brain and cellular change, has led to a shift in my approach to my professional practice as well as my own recovery.

* * * * *

Work with internal Parts and exploration of the images and experiences of our personal landscape can offer us a powerful base from which to heal. As we *listen* to their stories of meaning with compassion, our Parts will help us uncover the pathway to FLOWING recovery. Through our caring connection to those experiences, we can access Self-energy and the tools needed for empowerment in relationships across the lifespan.

Notes

1. Sakyong Mipham, *The Shambhala Principle: Discovering Humanity's Hidden Treasure* (New York: Harmony, 2013), 13–22.

2. Allan N. Schore, *Affect Regulation and the Origin of the Self: The Neurobiology of Emotional Development* (Hillsdale, NJ: Lawrence Earlbaum Assoc., 1994), 9–18.

3. Eckhart Tolle, *The Power of Now: A Guide to Spiritual Enlightenment* (Novato, CA: New World, 1999), 50.

4. Ibid.

5. Jon Kabat-Zinn, PhD, *Full Catastrophe Living: Using the Wisdom of Your Body and Mind to Face Stress, Pain, and Illness* (New York: Bantam Books, 1990), 277–410.

One world to share, one Earth to cherish.

six

OPEN HEART: FLOWING ACCEPTANCE

Recovery Artist

After the turmoil of loss at my mother's death, we sought out our vacation spot at a small, beautiful lake in the northwoods of Minnesota. One morning as the family slept, I escaped to the dock and pulled out my battered copy of The Artist's Way[1] *and the notebooks I'd filled two years earlier with my responses to the exercises offered within.*

As I reviewed one entry—a five-year plan that took account of no practical impediments, just my hopes—I was amazed to discover that the fifty items had nearly all been completed. I had not revisited the list after recording it, but my intentions had somehow come into being without conscious effort.

That morning brought me to an awareness of the continued movement of my energies, even while I'd had my back turned. I'd heard about consciousness expanding, but only fleeting glimpses had been available from my previously restricted perspective. Rules and roles, loss and fear had driven my hypervigilant nervous system, and I'd worked a lifetime to keep those fears from catching up to me. Now, that effort seemed futile. I could no longer perform according to what others might want me to be.

This expansive point of view opened new pathways for exploration. From that moment forward, as a self-proclaimed "recovery artist," I embraced all creative avenues, all forms of Self-leadership, within one simple phrase. The bushel basket of my anxiety lifted to let my little light of new-found wisdom shine. No more "others can do it/ say it/ be it better than I." I could finally claim my personal authority and own it.

It was not lost on me that this ah-ha moment came in the midst of grief; timing is not haphazard in life. When I laid claim to my new title, I realized I'd long been carrying a moniker with meaning for my life's work: my name, Ellen Claire. Chosen by my parents for its Irish ancestral roots, it means "clear light." What a lovely gift of ancestry and destiny I'd received. The unfolding universe was guiding me down a preordained path and purpose: lighting the way for others on their recovery journeys.

Mindful meditation can help you release and transform what limits you.

As we move through the practice of FLOWING, we *find* and *feel* the physical expression of our emotions in order to *listen* mindfully. But only through *open*-heartedness can we effectively engage the meanings held in the bodymind. When we *open* our hearts to elements of meaning that may arise from internal or external sources, we gain a unique opportunity for Self-knowledge.

From the nonjudgmental stance of an *open* heart, we invite pain and loss to our conscious awareness, where they can be explored and soothed without shame. Once we bring our vulnerable Parts to light, we can appreciate them for their protective roles and best-effort responses. We can then apply to our healing new-found energies that might otherwise be held in check for fear of a recurrence of past hurt. And with an *open* heart-space, we can enhance positive connections with our present-day life experiences.

With an open *heart-space,*
we can enhance positive connections
with our present-day
life experiences.

To access our blocked energies in their stored form—in essence, to figure out the way in and *open* a path for the way out—we must turn to our bodies. More than a mere container for the Self, the body is part of an intricately woven tapestry of individual expression of that Self. Mindfully engaging our physical being—or "embodied mindfulness"—informs our perspectives and allows us to participate in life.

Of course, mindfulness cannot prevent our bodies from aging or succumbing to disease. But embodied awareness offers transformative opportunities, including improved functioning of our immune system and targeted change in physical and emotional vitality. Beyond these direct consequences, embodied mindfulness offers peace in the midst of suffering, allowing our focus to shift to the gifts that remain rather than the opportunities, functions, or relationships that have been lost.

Enhancing the connections between physical awareness and emotional awareness requires active practice. Regular opportunities to attend to breath in the practice of meditation, along with engagement of the spinal column through a dignified posture, offer access to all parts of the body through the neural structures that intersect there, literally *opening* the physical pathways of internal connection. Whether we envision those connective energies as chakras, as dispassionate muscle groups, as joints holding pain, or as internalized Parts of the Self-system, it is important to seek their function and purpose.

Pain is a call for awareness, yet the tendency is to pull away, to actively resist pain through the use of medication, or to seek an external "fix" to what is wrong. If instead we first allow awareness and understanding to arise, we can learn what is being communicated through that medium, potentially leading to opportunity for release.

In many cases, such practice is likely to relieve the source of stress so disease may be forestalled and health engaged. But should there be a need for more direct "Western" medical intervention, this enhanced awareness can support and inform advocacy efforts for participation in our own healing and maintenance of our quality of life—urgent matters during times of chronic pain and life-threatening illness.

EMBODIED FLOWING

Opportunities to include the body in therapeutic awareness can be enhanced and expressed through movement practices such as yoga, dance, and tai-chi; through energy-releasing techniques such as massage and energy field therapies; and through active targeted movements such as in strength training or physical therapy.

Take a moment right now to stretch and breathe. As you move, remember to include elements of FLOWING by engaging in the *feeling* of expanded and contracted muscles. Note the moment of resistance, and stop there to *listen* to whether your muscles are ready to relax further or need you to hold steady where you are. *Opening* your heart to an awareness of past experiences and your fears for the future will better inform your decision making and engender compassion. Then, as explained in the next chapter, you'll be able to *witness* the limitations and amazing strengths of your unique physical being—without judgment.

Attention to FLOWING offers opportunities to express gratitude for your body's work, carrying you though life with grace despite the many demands on your physical structures and processes. Awareness of the moment-by-moment experiences of muscle contraction and release, especially those related to your heart and lungs, can offer options for best functioning at a level far beyond what even the most skilled healer can access through standard medical treatment.

Knowledge of optimal conditioning, attention to the influence of stress on the body, and efforts to strengthen and support physical systems all contribute to a lived relationship with the total experience of Self. Such awareness empowers and energizes each of us to be our best and to celebrate all that is available to us for physical and emotional expression.

CHAKRAS: EMBODIED ENERGY

Humankind has always struggled to understand its own purpose and place in the greater scheme of life. All religions, all philosophies, all spiritual practices have emerged in response to this eternal quest for meaning.

In today's interconnected world, and in view of all our complexities as humans, where do we go for the answers to our own existential questions?

A long-recognized effective approach that also offers tools for Self-awareness and healing can be found in the chakras: a system of meaning-making based on our embodied experience.[2] Hindu spiritualists recognize chakras as bodily centers—seven in all—that take in and give out energy. The chakras, as will become apparent in the discussion below, are named for their location in the body as well as their function.

In the chakra system, the seven bodily centers are located along the median, or midline, of the head and trunk of the body. Each center relates to a particular type of energy expression and, from an anatomical perspective, corresponds to endocrine and organ structures with particular physiologic functions in our bodies.

Through chakra awareness, we can apply a "*listening* cone" to each of the seven energy points, compassionately *opening* to the experiences and meanings held there. Channeling mind, body, and spirit together in this way allows for the expression and release of toxic elements, or ideas, that may be held within. Reduction of stress and expression of meanings can have powerful implications across our emotional, spiritual, relational, and physical functioning.

Although I was originally skeptical about "new-age" concepts such as chakra energy centers, my personal experience of a powerful energy shift after completing a yoga session connected me with a strong sense of the usefulness of chakra awareness in healing practices.

In an effort to better access the chakra system as a potential healing tool, I decided to engage it actively in my personal movement routine. After my standard stretching exercises, I "held" the energy from the session between my raised hands and then slowly lowered my arms along the sides of my head and body, stopping at various points along the way. As I focused on each of these critical points in the chakra field, I was amazed to feel a physical sensation of release and expansion. It was startling to notice a change of energy akin to a temperature shift as I moved through the different phases.

At another yoga practice session, I noticed that while lying flat in *suvana*, or corpse pose, my attention was drawn to the way different notes resonated in particular places along the center line of my body and face. My personal experience of *opening* to the energies of the chakras convinced me that it would have value for my clients as well.

Root Chakra

The first chakra, found at the base of the pelvic bowl, is essential to grounding and balanced functioning. Its location at the bottom of the spine connects it to the most fundamental aspects of life: digestion and elimination.

As a species, we unfortunately tend to isolate and attach shame-filled meanings to the functioning of root chakra organs, creating a troublesome disconnect across internal and external energy systems that may manifest itself in the form of eating and digestive disorders, or in the use of substances in compulsive and unhealthy patterns. Consider what might happen if, instead of ignoring or dismissing these basic functions, we took time to acknowledge their importance for not only our healthy physical functioning but also for our emotional and spiritual well-being.

Sacral Chakra

The second chakra, located below the navel, is the source of sexual and reproductive energies. This chakra is arguably the most problematic across cultures, and, perhaps as a result, is often unbalanced in individuals. This area is notable for its location at the lowest level of the vagus nerve, where depersonalization is at its most extreme, as happens in dissociation from life-threatening danger.

Because of its direct connection to sexual energies and identity, sacral chakra expression is restricted by social mores, double standards, and religious codes. The resulting lack of awareness, and of appropriate expression, often leads to blocked relationships within the Self-structure and with the world at large. Confused communications filled with double-bind messages disrupt male/female relationships in many societies. Denial of "feminine" emotions in favor of "masculine" displays of strength set up abusive relationship models in patriarchal systems.

Limitations of power become institutionalized as the devaluation of women in their fullest expression of being. Resulting limitations to personal identity development have far-reaching implications across genders and generations. Such disruptions are certainly a source of much misery in "man's inhumanity to man (and woman)," as is clearly demonstrated in sexual abuse and violence. These limitations are all the more ironic given that the sacral chakra is essentially the womb—the source of life and the most basic element of relationship-based, as well as biological, functioning.

Power Chakra

The third chakra is at the solar plexus, just below the ribcage. It involves the large diaphragm muscle that controls the breath. In our high-stress environment, this chakra often overfunctions in its role as defender and boundary monitor. Blockages and excesses in this chakra are rampant and are contributors to health concerns related to kidney, liver, pancreatic, and adrenal functioning.

These organs are compromised by the overextended autonomic nervous system in the "fight or flight" mobilization response to perceived threat. Digestive processes, fatigue, ulcers, and addictions may relate to an imbalance of the power chakra. Anger and rage indicate extremes at one end of this energy center, while submission and enabling represent the opposite polarity. Balance in this energy field will support healthy relationship boundaries and the ability to identify and communicate them effectively.

Heart Chakra

The center point and fulcrum of the chakra system is located at the heart chakra. Herein is found opportunity for clarity of emotion and *openness* in the bodymind. As the primary source of compassion and empathy, this chakra determines our overall successful balance, or imbalance, throughout the energy field. In Eastern philosophies, the heart is viewed as the place where the mind resides, and the two concepts are often encompassed by the same word.

The heart chakra bridges the lower and upper parts of the chakra system, connecting physical functioning with emotional and spiritual aspects and energies. It is expressed in the delicate balance between Self and other, between fulfillment and sacrifice.

As the organ that supplies energy to all other parts of the body, the heart either allows us to engage in a social encounter or, by its circulation and pace, prevents access. If the heartbeat is rapid, we are in a state of hyperarousal that inhibits our ability to process information beyond the "fight/flight" or "freeze" functions of the autonomic nervous system. From a state of calm *open-heartedness*, however, we can access and engage meaningfully with our own and others' essential goodness.

The heart chakra is accessible to most of us as a point of intervention and awareness. I often ask clients to "see" their experiences and emotions through the window of their *open* heart. When we engage in curiosity about meanings, I remind them to make a welcoming space in their heart and to invite Parts to share in their heart energy. In my own practice of meditation, I often exhale with the image of my heart sending out energy across space to those who may be in need of compassion. Truly the fourth chakra is the *open* heart of healing.

Throat Chakra

Located at the base of the throat, between the collarbones, the fifth chakra is a source of Self-expression and Self-representation. Communication through creative channels resides in the throat chakra and requires expression to achieve balance. When we are prevented from speaking our truth due to fear or in the name of social correctness, it is often in conflict with our own best interest. To find balance, it is essential for us to represent our needs and express our meanings across the range of physical and emotional experiences.

Unfortunately, many people judge themselves as lacking "talent" or being undeserving of the opportunity for such expression, and they restrict their activities accordingly. But although they may define their creative output as unworthy of display, what is really compromised is the opportunity to know and value the Self. Trauma victims, especially, tend to limit such expression, literally "choking" back their feelings and personal narratives as somehow "wrong." When such blocked stories eventually emerge, they are typically found to be made up of dangerous secrets relating to experiences of victimization.

Chronic levels of thyroid problems, stiff necks, and sore throats may be the outcome of imbalance in throat chakra energies. Unblocking can be practiced through acts of creative expression like singing, writing, and visual arts. The ability to clearly state one's ideas without need for permission, or fear of consequence, indicates an *open* and balanced throat chakra.

Third Eye Chakra

The sixth chakra is called the third eye. According to the ancients, this energy center is located between the eyebrows, at the middle of the forehead. Associated with the brain and the nervous system, this "eye" looks inward as one engages in a process of Self-discovery.

The key to finding balance through wisdom and insight, the third eye chakra provides energy for inspiration and imagination. Blocked energies at this location might be indicated by migraine headaches or sinus issues. Time spent on establishing or restoring Self-trust is necessary allow the third eye to see past the blockage and begin to access recovery from traumatic loss.

Crown Chakra

The seventh chakra is the crown, the highest point of both the body and the emotional/spiritual state of Self-actualization. Located above the head at the point of extension of the spinal column's energy, this area of higher spiritual concern and awareness is associated with an understanding of our place the larger universe. These energies are expressed in higher states of consciousness, beyond self-involvement or personal gain, extending outward to where we are all part of a larger truth.

Blockages in this chakra may manifest as nervous disorders and emotional illnesses. Balanced energies will be found in social responsibility and compassionate participation in the world.

Blockages in the crown chakra may manifest as nervous disorders and emotional illnesses.

The crown chakra is dependent on access to the entire chakra system. It would be impossible to balance the crown's energy without *opening* up overall balance throughout the system.

CHAKRA ALIGNMENT AND HEALING

My personal experiences with chakra energy centers led me to begin asking my clients about the sensations they felt in their bodies, and the locations of those sensations, as they identified emotional reactions to life events. Often, my clients spontaneously expressed the conjoined nature of their emotional and physical sensations without my questioning.

Clients reported a variety of physical sensations: "blinding headaches" when dealing with sensitive issues of self-awareness; a choking or blocked feeling in trying to verbalize a thought; breathlessness in times of fear; physical pain from the "heartache" of betrayal; feeling "punched in the gut" by powerlessness; nausea in response to interpersonal loss; and abdominal pain or numbness when talking about life-threatening incidents. In each instance, they reported an energy constriction in a particular chakra center.

Even more striking were clients' reports of physical manifestations of pain or disease taking form within the organs of related centers—including autoimmune disorders such as lupus and fibromyalgia, migraines, cancers, and reproductive and digestive disorders. These manifestations were much too frequently found among the child-abuse victims in my practice and in the practices of my therapist colleagues to be disregarded.

When I later learned of the polyvagal theory,[3] the pieces of the jigsaw puzzle suddenly began to fall into place for me.

The polyvagal theory—developed after intensive study of the central nervous system and its workings—explains the functioning of the vagus nerve of the brain, the largest cranial nerve. The vagus nerve extends down along the right side of the neck and then branches out around the heart and the lungs, into the abdomen, and along the spine, affecting every part of the human body.

The polyvagal system functions as a safety monitor and has profound implications for human relationships and physical survival. In a rapid-fire determination, it offers us guidance on whether to participate in a social relationship in order to facilitate connection and meaning-making, to resist or escape the interaction, or to shut down completely if a situation poses a perceived life threat without options for escape.

The vagus nerve has branches extending to every organ, including the hormone-releasing organs of the endocrine system that control the fight-flight-freeze response, just as there are such organs at or near each of the chakra points. Of course, healers of old who applied the "mystical" concept of chakras had more limited awareness of the anatomy and physiology of the human body. But when viewed through the lens of polyvagal theory, the ancient wisdom of chakra energy systems holds more truth—and more inherent value in explaining the bodymind in action—than might first meet the eye.

---

* * * * *

Open-hearted, nonjudgmental attention to the subtleties of the bodymind can expand our options for recovery from trauma and loss. Using the ancient system of chakra energy awareness, we can engage our own internal wisdom and inherent tendency toward balance. These resources can further our efforts to access FLOWING health in mind, body, and spirit.

Notes

1. Julia Cameron, *The Artist's Way: A Spiritual Path to Higher Creativity* (New York: Penguin, 1992).

2. C. W. Leadbeater, *The Chakras* (Wheaton, IL: Theosophical Printing, 1927).

3. Stephen Porges, *The Polyvagal Theory: The Neurophysiological Foundation of Emotions, Attachment, Communication & Self-Regulation* (New York: Norton, 2011), 52–61.

Each of us is the sum of many parts—working together for safety and strength.

seven

WITNESS: EMPATHIC FLOWING

A-maz-ing Revelations

Years after my cancer diagnosis, a job I'd enjoyed and done well ended badly. I'd been reluctant to take the job in the first place, fearing that the heavy demands might threaten my recovery. I realized, however, that hiding from challenges was no way to move ahead, so I'd accepted the offer. But after I'd spent three years in the position, personality conflicts had created a toxic environment, so I resigned. The process of disentangling myself was filled with hostility and recrimination and, along with some family transitions, triggered a full-blown state of PTSD.

I wish I could report that, in response to the sleepless nights and obsessive self-doubt that overwhelmed me during this period, I immediately sought professional help. But in honesty, I withdrew to "tend my wounds" and tried to just get on with life. To my good fortune, several months after the job trauma I learned of a weekend retreat for breast cancer survivors. The retreat, a major turning point in my recovery, required me to face up to self-defeating thoughts and behaviors, to look deeply into myself to access resources I'd never known I had, and to take ownership of my recovery effort.

Among the powerful transitions that occurred during that weekend was my introduction to the labyrinth on the retreat grounds. As I mindfully walked the labyrinth's stone-lined path, my self-limiting perspective opened to something deeper and more connected across time and space. Somehow, entering that sacred circle brought me to a greater awareness of my capacity to choose my path in a loving and compassionate internal landscape. My lifelong tendency to seek approval from others loosed its choke-hold as it became clear to me that this practice only set me up as a screen for their projections. This simple foray on a winding path led me home to myself.

I've returned to the labyrinth several times since that weekend, each time coming away with new realizations. One visit offered an awareness of the similarity of that iconic image to the whorls and turnings of the human brain. I couldn't help but consider the mindful applications of this archetypal structure to accessing and rewiring crossed or misconnected neural pathways.

As I wound through the maze, each step I took in a Self-aware compassionate state seemed to unknot my former self-limiting pattern and clarify my internal resources. During occasional pauses, I looked up and became aware of some new delight in my external environment. My ever-vigilant hawk-guide multiplied by three in the blue sky above my head; the sound of children's laughter emanated from a nearby back yard; the trees surrounding the retreat center grounds seemed to dance as springtime winds freshened the air. After each experience at the labyrinth, I felt a surge of gratitude and a sense of well-being.

*****

My fear of losing touch with the magic of the place keeps me from visiting the labyrinth more regularly. But the labyrinth's inspiration continues in my life in many forms: through my art, my work, and my day-to-day contact with those around me. I try to bring that labyrinthine perspective to my daily journey of recovery, always curious about what new discovery might be around the next corner.

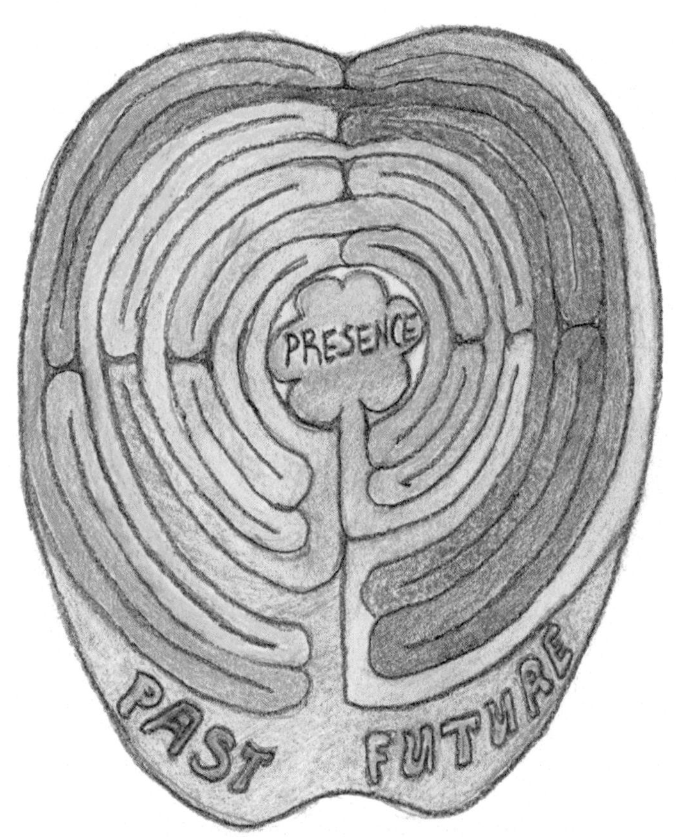

We are interconnected beings in a labyrinth of relationships and meanings.

Emotional healing is more than just a change of attitude. It requires a fundamental shift to a more secure level of attachment; the end result of this shift is improved *integration* of bodymind systems.

This deep level of healing requires that we act as *witness* to the experiences and meanings that make up our lives. Active *witnessing* calls for a willingness to recognize that every child is inherently deserving of safety, nurturing, and love.

Our most fundamental human need is to be seen and heard by another. It is through the "eye of the beholder" that we gain a perspective on who we are in the world; but if that reflection is distorted, compassionately bearing *witness* to our own experience is our best opportunity for recovery.

Often, the most significant point in healing is when the energy of Self is applied to truly *witnessing* the lessons learned in developmental trauma. Compassionate attention to significant events in our history can clean the site of internal wounds and make healing possible.

Compassionate attention to significant events can clean the site of internal wounds and make healing possible.

Trauma researchers were among the first to emphasize *witnessing* as crucial to recovery. Telling the secrets of a dysfunctional family history or disclosing shame-filled actions has often been found to bring a measure of relief, yet the path is inevitably full of roadblocks and U-turns. In early trauma therapy efforts, clinicians and their traumatized clients seemed to be stumbling around in dark caves, trying to find their way through the healing process without any concept of the size or shape of the hidden terrain. Failures were inevitable, and the resulting shift to evidence-based treatment was a positive step.

Until recently, identifying evidence-based treatment was limited by the practical difficulties of measuring abstract concepts and the often elusive elements of emotional change. Now, with sophisticated technologies to measure and map the brain and nervous system, there is finally a light through the tunnel—a way to see the effects of serving as *witness* to one's own story. By allowing us to establish a calm, receptive base and regulate our emotional responses, active *witnessing* fosters enhanced neural *integration* and improves our general health.

SOMATIC THERAPIES

Mind/body connections are being explored widely through currently popular practices in wellness and nutrition. Even more striking, however, is the evidence of those connections within mental health and trauma treatment models. Somatic (from the Latin root *soma*, or body) models attend to emotion via movement and awareness of the "unspoken voice" of bodily expressions.[1] The interconnectedness of nervous system–based responses to past security threats and how the meanings of those events are held can be complex. But accessing those stored responses creates opportunity to ease our struggles and work toward true *integration*.

Through somatic therapies, we can avoid the retraumatizing effects of many exposure therapies. If we calmly *witness* the body and the emotional signals the body receives, we can bypass some of the more jarring aspects of pain and loss. Put differently, we can recognize and attend to the physical/emotional discomfort before delving into traumatic meanings or distorted cognitive explanations. This gentler way into the *integration* of traumatic experiences offers a measure of release even before the trauma narrative is known.

Among the truths that are supported by neuroscience and psychotherapy are the following:

- **We are interconnected.** Human development requires interaction with other primary figures. The infant brain will not develop effectively unless it has another, more mature person's brain to "tap into." This interpersonal exchange has a natural extension to therapeutic relationships and recovery.
- **Development is embodied and multileveled, as is healing.** Information is taken in and processed on visual, auditory, spatial, temporal, cognitive, experiential, emotional, chemical, energetic, and universal levels—to name a few. The adage "actions speak louder than words" barely begins to address the truth.
- **We learn and heal best in a calm state.** Stress communicates to the nervous system a lack of safety, limiting information processing to only those elements related to basic survival (fight, flight, or freeze). Mixed messages such as those found in abusive or traumatic events are sorted at the most fundamental level—our best hope for escape or reduction of threat. Only when the environment is deemed safe is the healing influence of social receptivity available.
- **Mindfulness is a powerful healing tool.** Practices that allow for calm focus provide the best environment for targeted change. Self-awareness is key to supporting and maintaining mental health. Through such

nonjudgmental awareness of distorted meanings, attachment based models-of-self can be reorganized to healthier patterns.

- **The brain and body continually change.** Changes—such as immune system activity and mental health recovery—occur through neuroplasticity and cellular regeneration, and can be fostered by calm, focused attention to specific, targeted areas within emotional and physical systems.
- **Trauma and recovery have multigenerational implications.** Suffering creates patterns, influences, and adaptations across generations, causing not only behavioral changes but also genetic changes that may leave later generations more vulnerable. Participation in regular mindfulness activities has been found to similarly affect genetic expression toward greater flexibility and improved mental and physical health.

PATHWAYS TO FLOWING

The way of recovery is a winding path, and the options available to trauma victims to explore and *witness* are many and varied. Some options may be sustained as ongoing practice, whereas others may be transformed or discarded along the way.

Rather than regard the abandonment of a practice—even after a period of meaningful exploration—as loss or a failure, the trauma survivor should consider it to be the next step of the journey to healing. Each effort can build on the accomplishments of the previous one as we develop new skills on the path to recovery.

As I write these words, I reflect on the stepping stones of my own recovery process. Through a physical-emotional lens, I am conscious of my procession from sedentary teen through adoption of a yoga practice to bring balance to my days; my dual lives as a professional and a mother demanded it. Abrupt change was wrought by the hydra-headed beast: cancer. There my journey derailed into multiple demands of survival—surgery, chemotherapy, and radiation—while I still tried to maintain my personal and professional lives. Frantic efforts to counter and soothe those ravages and manage those challenges drove my quest to find alternative and complementary opportunities.

In addition to exploring alternative recovery options such as acupuncture, chiropractic care, nutrition, massage, and physical therapies, I pursued more emotionally therapeutic options. Survival-specific workshops and retreats offered a new sense of hope and intention toward mindful living. Timing was providential in the form of new discoveries in brain-based interventions and interpersonal neurobiology. Research and training in these areas clarified my direction and confirmed the effectiveness of Self-led efforts. Nowhere was this more true for me than in the turmoil of grief following personal loss, which led me to train in Internal Family Systems (IFS) work and practice.

Along with attention to bodymind healing, I dedicated energy to renewing the environment. Efforts to live and eat more holistically led me to a stronger sense of my body's nutritional needs and centered my efforts to consume whole foods and to connect with the Earth more effectively by shopping, preparing, and composting, as well as attending to water-management practices through collection barrels and a native plant rain garden. As each effort is fine-tuned, I gradually access the most effective approaches for participation in my personal journey of recovery.

Opportunities to explore within our own particular means and environment are unlimited. Curiosity and self-compassion will guide such explorations as long as we *open* our hearts and bear *witness*. Sustained efforts to bodymind healing can lead us to more secure attachment status and improved coping in the face of challenges.

SELF-REGULATION

Along with instilling a sense of competence in a child, the benefits of secure attachment include supporting the development of a skill set known as emotional Self-regulation. Self-regulation is the ability to step back from an initial reactive response to an issue or event and to instead respond from a more considered, or moderate, position. The opposite of Self-regulation is emotional instability, which at its most extreme might present as mental illness.

Having a "secure base" early in life is a major contributor to the capacity for Self-regulation. However, we can still access this ability later in life by compassionately *witnessing* the way our Parts cope. Maintaining a nonjudgmental stance—allowing us to avoid the disruptive influences of shame and self-doubt that might arise from evaluation—supports emotional Self-regulation.

We can access Self-regulation later in life by witnessing *the way our Parts cope.*

As we bear *witness* to our Parts' vulnerability in moments of trauma, it is important for us to maintain an awareness of the natural, rapid-fire nature of the adaptation and coping that were required in the moment of trauma. Attending to their story with an *open* heart validates and normalizes the intense experience, whereas questioning fosters expectations of blame. Every Part needs to be assured of our respect for the effort, if not the outcome of the events that they had to cope with for the sake of survival.

Even Parts that seem destructive have a protective function behind their roles. Reassuring these Parts that we know they *did the best they could with whatever resources were available in an unpredictable situation* will invite continued access. Celebrating every Part for contributing to the management of a chaotic situation—and surviving it—provides a strong foundation for continued recovery.

Stepping Back

There are several elements of Self-regulation in recovery that correspond to aspects of the FLOWING model. Initially, it is necessary to notice emotions, *feeling* them as they arise in the bodymind. This can be a challenge since protective Parts often block our awareness of uncomfortable experiences. But if we notice, then *open* some space to internally step back from our reaction—perhaps by shifting our awareness to calm breathing—we will find it possible to *listen* without being overwhelmed.

When I first heard the doctor say I had breast cancer, I experienced a strong impulse to try to escape the room to avoid the need to take on the frightening implications of that diagnosis. If I had acted on that impulse, however, it would have taken me away from my best hope of recovery—treatment planning with my medical team.

Instead, I calmed myself and used my resources to stay present and aware of my treatment options—knowing that later, I could spend time with my emotions, acknowledging and expressing them in a safe and effective way. This is an example of Self-regulation in action.

It is important not to disengage, instead maintaining a presence just at the edge of our discomfort with what's happening—essentially to "sit with it" and see what happens. Engaging with curiosity is another way to *witness* what our Parts hold.

Self-Representation

Witnessing does not mean merely observing our Parts in their struggle to cope with fear and loss. We also must support their release of trauma-based emotions. Overwhelming fears require expression and representation. We can tap into our emotions using creativity and *listen* mindfully to what experiences mean and how they could be best addressed to find resolution.

The way information is released in the bodymind can sometimes surprise us. Neuroscience has identified some forms of release to take note of in the acronyms SIFT (sensations, images, feelings, and thoughts)[2] and SIBAM (sensation, image, behavior, affect, and memory).[3] Each listed area for attention refers to the nervous system's symbolic and somatic (bodymind) representation of meaningful information. By applying these descriptions to broaden the way we *witness* our internal Parts, we may discover the richness of meanings they hold and find creative ways to unburden from trauma.

When traumatic meanings are *witnessed*, acknowledged, and offered release through the energy channels of the bodymind, Parts are given space to take in new information about their roles. Taking every opportunity to represent our belief in and gratitude for the protective efforts of Parts—even as we may strive to find more effective ways for that protection to be managed—builds strength in those internal relationships. The Self may then be trusted to monitor threats and regulate further emotional upheaval, lessening reactivity and enhancing Self-regulation.

*****

Neuroplasticity and our amazingly adaptive minds and bodies ensure that what is *witnessed* in our internal explorations expands opportunities for growth. What we remain *open* to, guides our healing journey; what we resist or try to control, intensifies the challenge. A conscious effort to apply the FLOWING model to Self-regulation offers us access to some of the most effective remedies available on our recovery journeys.

Notes

1. Peter A. Levine, *In an Unspoken Voice: How the Body Releases Trauma and Restores Goodness* (Berkeley, CA: North Atlantic Books, 2010), 73–95.

2. Daniel J. Siegel, *Pocket Guide to Interpersonal Neurobiology: An Integrative Handbook of the Mind* (New York: Norton, 2012), 17.

3. Peter A. Levine, *Trauma and Memory: Brain and Body in a Search for the Living Past: A Practical Guide for Understanding and Working with Traumatic Memory* (Berkeley, CA: North Atlantic Books, 2015) 46–50.

THE THIRD PART

SUSTAINED FLOWING

The practice of FLOWING is a call to action from a deep level of Self, asking us to engage compassionately with our internal Parts and their stories of past experiences and hurts. By exploring the attachment-based meanings that are at the core of our identity, we can revise them and incorporate them in their updated form.

This third part of the book focuses on how we can purposefully direct our actions to support and reorganize the meanings that define us. After "weeding out" the misinformation sown by unmet needs for safety and recognition, we must feed and water the elements that remain and plant new seeds. By further developing our practice of FLOWING, we provide support to newly established neural structures, allowing them to put down roots and eventually blossom into Self-energy and recovery.

With intention and effort, *integration* allows our Self-energy to expand, going beyond habit changes to open up the nervous system to new opportunities for personal development. Accordingly, chapter eight explains the I in FLOWING, *integration*—what it is, why it is so important, and how we can achieve it.

Chapter nine explores the N in FLOWING: *nurturing*. We *nurture* ourselves by making a commitment to the care and feeding of our healthy personal growth. *Nurturing* is extended though the regular practice of daily activities that, by strengthening our sense of safety and predictability, help promote recovery. Celebrations of life events and milestones, along with intentional rituals, become opportunities to *nurture* and promote bodymind and spiritual healing.

Finally, chapter ten discusses the last letter in FLOWING, G, which stands for *generativity*. In this more expansive stage of life and recovery, our focus shifts from ourselves to the world and people around us. By sharing ourselves, our talents, and our time with others, we *generate* new opportunities for healing in the larger community. When our recovery efforts are grounded in Self-energy and compassion, we plant new seeds with the potential to promote healing on a global scale.

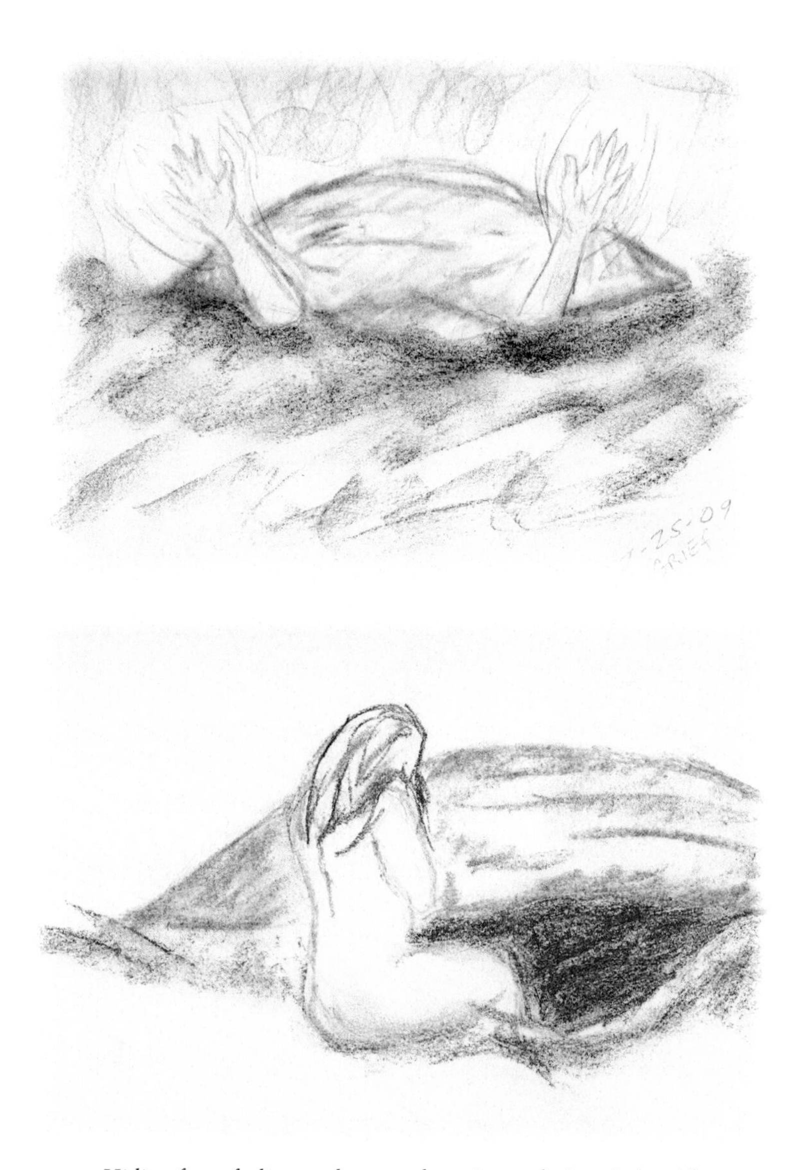

Hiding from feelings only traps them. Instead, sit quietly with what emerges, acknowledge it, and let it go.

eight
INTEGRATE: EMBRACING FLOWING

The Grandmother Guide

It had been a rough spring and summer for me. I'd spent countless hours at the hospital bedside of my eldest sister, Mary Kay, whose cancer treatment had caused damage from which she couldn't recover. I'd been called away from an Internal Family Systems (IFS) training weekend to be with her at her passing. My shock and grief as she lost the fight against our common nemesis were profound.

Six weeks later, I attended another IFS training weekend. Our days started with a short internal check-in to connect with our Parts—those protectors and holders of emotion that emerge in response to everyday interactions and events, shaping our perspectives and coloring our responses. On this particular day, the check-in was a guided "path exercise" requiring us to visualize a pathway that we'd walked at some point in our lives.

The familiar path I saw was the road outside our family's summer vacation cabin. In my mind, I thought to cross the road to a logging trail in the forest preserve behind the cabin to investigate where it would lead. But against this conscious plan, I discovered that I was walking up the gravel drive toward the cabin. Even as I tried to correct my direction, I heard the group leader's voice instructing that we would soon reach a structure—perhaps a temple or a cabin, she suggested.

My observing Self marveled at the rightness of my initial impulse, as I relaxed into the familiar action of climbing the steps to the porch and reaching for the screen door. "There," I heard the leader tell us, "you will encounter your guide." Without missing a beat, I stepped into the cabin's front room and saw my long-dead maternal grandmother, seated at the old oak table around which our family had enjoyed so many meals, conversations, and games over the years.

The experience of joyful reunion felt real to me, as Parts of my internal system took seats around the table, looking expectantly toward Gramma Cotten in anticipation of hearing her burbling Irish brogue. But I heard no words, seeing only images and impressions of rough seas and sensing fears and losses, as a journey across the ocean splashed into my consciousness.

I wondered where we were headed until a bright image flashed across my inner sight: silhouettes of a chain of women standing at the edge of the iconic Cliffs of Moher on Ireland's western coast. The exercise was over, but I knew I would learn more from this message as we shifted into the business of the training day.

* * * * *

This final weekend of IFS training was spiritually focused, designed to help us explore our internally held beliefs and sources of meaning. At times I experienced challenging triggers around recent losses, as well as memories of childhood injustices and exploitation. As I acknowledged the struggles of my Parts, much of my sense of being wronged virtually drained away, freeing an awareness of my own positive intentions from old snares of unwanted, undeserved shame. As I felt relief arise in waves around me, the Irish Cliffs again flashed before my internal eye, beckoning me toward further exploration.

The training weekend moved to a close with a sense of celebration and, for me, the knowledge that both my professional skills and my personal recovery had advanced to new levels. A celebration with music and an exchange of token gifts by our circle of trainees prepared us for our commencement ritual.

One member of our group passed around a box of laminated cards bearing images, mostly of dreamy goddess figures, with brief messages about mindfulness qualities. She invited us to sift through the box and take cards that spoke to us. I chose a few cards and then saw the word Patience *emblazoned on one card. It was a theme word for me, a quality that I'd been consciously striving to engage in my life. When I turned my eyes to the image on the front of the card I saw, once again, the Cliffs of Moher.*

* * * * *

The next morning, I carefully made time to learn whatever my guide wanted me to know about that haunting image of the cliffs. Returning my thoughts to the northwoods cabin and the old oak table, I meditated quietly in the comfortable chair that had been my mother's favorite refuge. I opened myself to the flow of images and meaning that might emerge from my uninterrupted exploration and requested guidance.

My request was answered quickly, and I found myself back on the rough waves of the Atlantic. My grandmother's only return to her native land had been in 1912, after she'd lived ten years in the US. In my internal vision, I traveled with Marie, docking at Queenstown (now Cobh'), Ireland, where we unloaded our large steamer trunks onto the back of an open, horse-drawn cart. Traveling over rough terrain, we reached the cliffs, where women of the family line were gathered, dressed in rough, home-

spun woolen garments and shawls. Each added her own trunk or carved wooden box to the stack on the cart, then followed along on foot as we proceeded northwest.

We arrived at my grandmother's birthplace in County Mayo—the place from which her grandfather had been driven by his Protestant Bishop landlord during the famine years in retribution for refusing to send his children to the Church of Ireland school. We then processed around the Partry Mountains to the home of my great-great-grandmother, where Marie had grown up separated from her younger siblings. It surprised me that the stop there was brief, with another box or two quickly added to the cart before we resumed our westward travels, beyond the shadow of Crogh Patrick, into a lunar landscape of windswept sandstone.

Finally, the cart stopped, and each traveler took her box from the rough-planked wagon bed and placed it at the foot of a small hill. I recognized the Celtic cross at the top of the hill, realizing that I'd discovered this lonely monument, dedicated to those who had died by the thousands during the mid-nineteenth century potato famine, on a trip to Ireland that I'd made years earlier.

As the women unloaded and stacked their boxes, I was aware of the common burdens of misfortune, mistreatment, and displacement—shared across untold generations of ancestors and filtered down through my mother to me. This opportunity to lay down those burdens to promote the healing of my entire lineage of mothers and grandmothers brought with it a strong sense of relief and clarity.

My part of the journey of unburdening was complete, but I understood that the process needed time to reach back into history. I mentally stepped away and reentered my conscious life, but I took time over the next several days to check in. As I did, I always saw more ancestors with more boxes, patiently waiting their turn to lay down the common burdens of misunderstandings and limited circumstance.

* * * * *

Ten days after these amazing revelations, I checked in again to see what progress had been made. My internal eye took in a huge stack of boxes, reminiscent in its shape and layers of an ancient Mayan pyramid, with the famine memorial at its apex. Only one figure remained to add her box to the collection. My initial confusion gave way to an awareness that this was my recently lost sister, resting her own version of the burden of missed opportunity at the pinnacle of the collection.

My gratitude for my sister's release—and that of all the mothers, sisters, and fellow travelers—from undeserved and unwanted burdens is abundant. It fuels my work, inspires my creativity, and fills my heart with hope.

Celebrate all that you have and all that you are.

FLOWING is not just an acronym; it is an adjective meaning to move with fluidity in a continuous direction. FLOWING is active even in stillness; it is knowing without restricting; it is curiosity as conscious effort but with no particular agenda.

What actually happens when we take the time to be in a calm, aware, nonjudgmental state? How can it help in the long run? I hear these questions frequently in my therapy practice—I asked them as well during my recovery from breast cancer. In its basic, pared-down form, the answer has to do with our ability to "own" our experiences and their meaning in the big picture we have of "Self." Ownership promotes a process of *integration* across physical, emotional, and perceptual levels. As we *feel*, *listen* with *open* hearts, and *witness* the burdens held by our "Parts," *integration* occurs naturally at the level of the nervous system.

In a holistic sense, health is a state of balance. Optimal health can be achieved only if biological and psychological elements work in tandem, not as separate entities. By contrast, illness and pain—whether emotional or physical—are evidence of imbalance.

Optimal health can be achieved only if biological and psychological elements work in tandem, not as separate entities.

As discussed in chapter one, infants are "wired" to form attachments to their caregivers. From their first moments of life outside the womb, newborns depend on their caregivers to guide and support their sense of Self-in-the-world. Early, secure attachment offers the most effective opportunity for *integration* on bio-psycho-social levels and establishes patterning for an individual's lifelong health. But if the developmental environment was threatening or unpredictable, such distressing information had to be isolated from awareness for the child to cope and to survive. As a result, these isolated, distressing elements were not effectively *integrated* in the child's autobiographical memory.

Integration is a process of bringing together elements of experience and awareness to create meaning and promote progress along the recovery path. Calm, nonjudgmental awareness—which is to say, the practice of mindfulness—eliminates physical-emotional disconnections and promotes *integration*.

For an example of the power of *integration*, look to the trees for inspiration, which literally means "to breathe in." As energy flows from earth and sky, the trees take it in and maintain flexibility. Trees flourish in good times and stand strong amidst storms. They endure, participating in the cycle of life without trying to grab control of their environment; give breath and take nourishment from their interconnection with living things around them; and create new growth from decay. They remain rooted in the earth until their time is complete.

But even then, they contribute to the warmth, shelter, and comfort of living beings. This ability to flexibly coexist and to contribute energy across many fields of interaction is *integration* at its fullest expression.

For individuals with severe mental and physical pain whose blocked, contained energies hold painful memories and meanings from intolerable events, the prospect of *opening* themselves to such awareness may be daunting. Why would anyone want to "attend" to such matters? But this is where the opportunity for nonjudgmental awareness is a powerful option. With appropriate guidance, regular practice of Self-awareness from a state of calm acceptance will produce changes in neural functioning and repair disrupted *integration*.

Regular practice of Self-awareness will produce changes in neural functioning and repair disrupted integration.

Interpersonal Neurobiology developer Dan Siegel has created a useful model for understanding *integration*.[1] He views *integration* as a river with two banks, one called Chaos and the other Rigidity, on either side of a body of active, moving water. This image is quite apt as a metaphor for life, with its constant currents and changing conditions that demand that we reorient ourselves and navigate to maintain a balanced state. Drifting too far to one shore can make us anxious or disorganized; the other side may bog us down into sluggish depression or stuck deep in our limitations. The challenge is to "glide along with the current" so as to use that energy to steer a clear, flexible course through the river of life while *integrating* the disruptions that may pull us off course.

HOW DOES INTEGRATION HAPPEN?

At the neural level, the brain and body hold on to real-world experiences of pain and fear in case new, similar events occur and

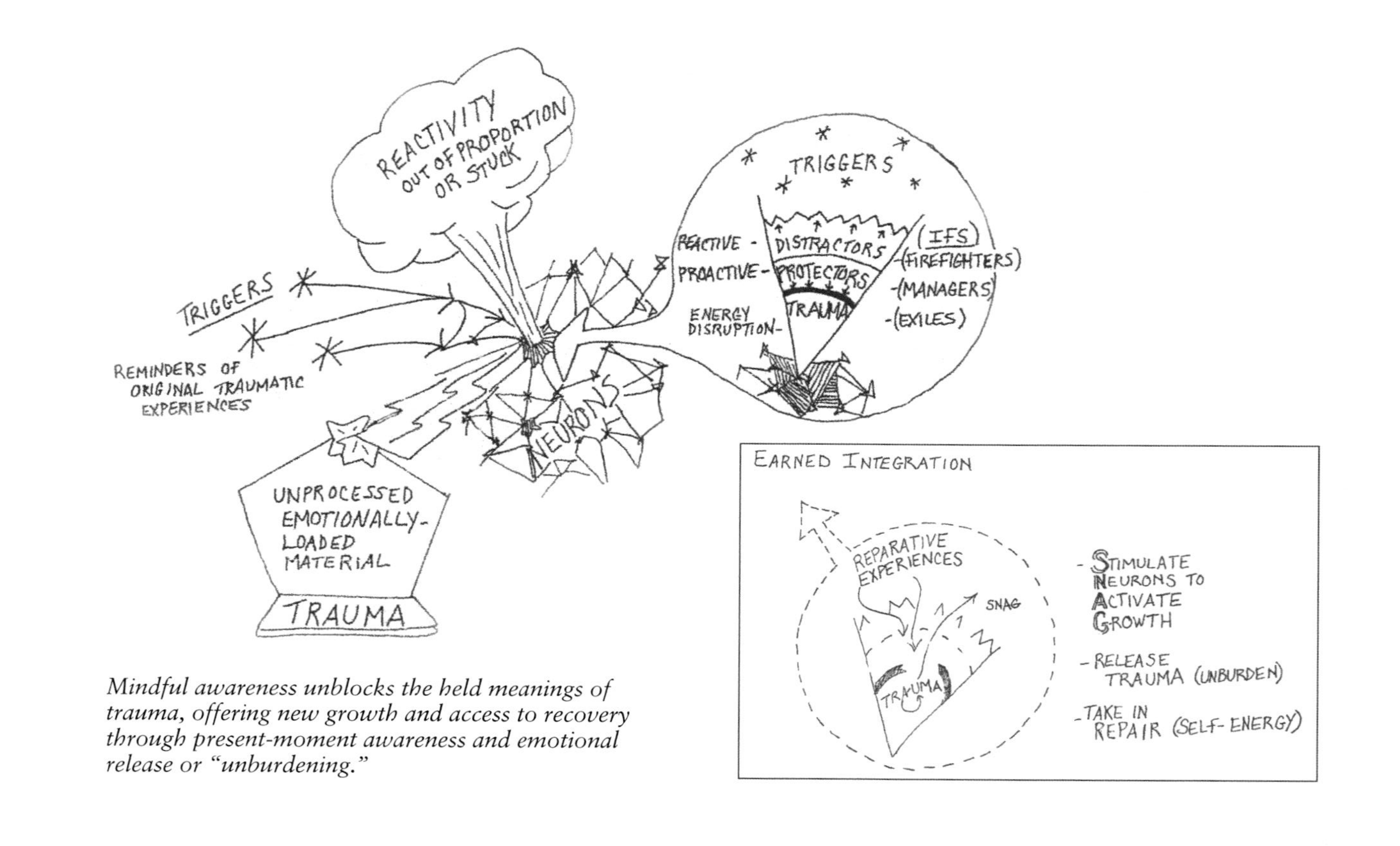

Mindful awareness unblocks the held meanings of trauma, offering new growth and access to recovery through present-moment awareness and emotional release or "unburdening."

quick responses are needed. This natural defense keeps information about an original trauma in an unprocessed, un*integrated* state, blocking the trauma victim's access to new relationship patterns or healing experiences.

For *integration* to take place, these defensive and protective aspects (Parts) must be approached respectfully and in a calm, safe environment. More intensive experiences of trauma are best explored in professional therapy to ensure appropriate support. The compassionate exploration of a traumatic event can allow the survivor to effectively bypass natural defenses and work toward *integration.*

In the illustration (left), notice the bundle labeled "trauma." Fear, pain, and unmet emotional needs that were isolated for the sake of survival occupy this bundle. Because of their unprocessed form, these active elements intrude into subsequent relationships.

A survivor's perception of the trauma is stuck in a time warp—unable to connect with the safety established by time and distance; so the survivor often responds to behaviors, places, or situations that bear even slight resemblance to the original traumatic events—"triggers"—as if they are of the same emotional magnitude as the earlier event. The mushroom cloud in the illustration signifies this extreme, overblown "reactivity" to triggers.

Next, look at the circle representing a close-up view of neurons holding trauma beneath protective/distracting response patterns, illustrating blocked receptivity to new information. The "earned *integration*" panel shows how mindful awareness unblocks the held meanings of trauma, offering new growth (SNAG)[2] and access to recovery through present-moment awareness and emotional release or "unburdening."

EMBODIED INTEGRATION

Internally focused, Self-led participation in mindful activity promotes repaired neural *integration* across activities and meanings, lending support to effective recovery. But the level of awareness that *integration* requires is impossible to sustain on a constant basis. Regular daily practices, such as yoga and meditation, can enhance the effectiveness of bodymind *integration*. Yoga—including muscle stretching and contracting, opening energy-body channels, and engaging with circulatory/respiratory systems—is an established model of *integrative activity*. Through regular yoga practice, neural pathways in the brain and body can be activated, creating stronger, healthier patterns of bodymind *integration*.

In addition to its clear physical benefits, *integration* increases Self-awareness, allowing the trauma survivor to better manage boundaries in relationships and more easily control reactions to conflict. Paying attention to physical and emotional energy prevents the buildup and blockages that might compromise natural healing or disrupt participation in relationships.

Integration increases Self-awareness, allowing the trauma survivor to better manage boundaries in relationships.

Conscious Awareness

Though conscious awareness—attention to the full experience of the present moment—disrupted *integration* can be repaired. "Neuroplasticity" allows for the creation of new connections in the brain and the redirection of cell functioning. These processes, when engaged appropriately, offer opportunities for change on mental, physical, and emotional levels.

—ꟺ—

Through conscious awareness,
disrupted integration
can be repaired.

—ꟺ—

To best capitalize on these change opportunities, visualization and other sensory abilities can be called on. This may include movement or tactile expression, music, singing or chanting for vocal and auditory stimulation, aroma therapy, and attention to flavors and textures. The options are only as limited as your range of expression.

Spinal Respiratory FLOWING

Working to achieve *integration* requires finding opportunities to reflect on the status of your bodymind; to check in with your Self-system; and to notice your environment, your physiology including posture and breathing, and your emotions and their related meanings. In short, *integration* requires actively engaging with all your mental and physical processes.

To foster *integration*, it is important to follow the breath and connect with the bodymind. Attention to posture supports communication between the peripheral nerves, which are responsible for voluntary movement and for autonomic (automatic) functions to keep body systems working effectively. The spine holds bundles of these extended nerves and allows them to communicate with the executive functions of the brain.

Intentional work with posture and movement is essential to *integrative* efforts.

Combining breath and body awareness in the present moment is a highly effective way to access *integration.* So take an upright posture, check in with your body, breathe in, and be inspired.

To help clients access the calm self-awareness that is essential to *integration,* I encourage them to seek out the answers to their questions about meaning and emotions from within. By exploring and understanding the deeply held meanings of traumatic and attachment-based experiences, we can help those Parts that carry emotional burdens achieve full expression and healing.

Working together in my office, I ask clients to begin by noticing their breathing—without judgment or thoughts of making changes. Drawing our attention to the calm instilled in the body by the supply of oxygen, we focus on the brow. This "third eye" chakra at the center of the frontal lobes of the brain is a natural starting place. The corpus callosum—the bundle of connecting fibers between the right (emotional/creative) and left (logical) hemispheres of the brain—is just behind that space, offering a natural bridge to accessing the bodymind. Furthermore, the amygdala, containing unprocessed emotions, is the "lamp" that lights our discoveries.

Picturing a lighthouse-like beam of focus, we scan the interior of the head and skull, descending slowly as if on a spiral staircase to gradually become aware of internal experiences or sensations. *Feeling* our way along, we *listen* for body-based communications of blocked or held energy—such as pain, numbness, or vibrations.

We pause together and breathe to acknowledge whatever presents before continuing and completing the scan. We pay specific attention to areas known to hold stress: the jaw muscles, neck and shoulders, and the chakra zones. Tracking nervous system pathways in and around the spine, we send intentional support and interest to the internal organs and bodily systems, and extend an invitation to our Parts to bring to conscious awareness conflicted meanings or withheld energy.

The body scan is completed by mentally discharging any accumulated tension through our legs, feet, arms, hands, and fingers. From that point, we reengage those more active or blocked places for further inquiry and exploration as we *open* to and *witness* from deeper levels of FLOWING.

Somatic Integration

Exposure to trauma and loss is an inevitable part of the human experience. The trauma response can be extreme, depending on whether we have opportunity to move through and grieve, or otherwise adapt to, these losses. Repeated exposure to overwhelming loss and limited options for safe recovery are factors that often result in post-traumatic stress disorder (PTSD) or other trauma-based disorders.

But with attention to *felt* sensations, we can encounter and express much of the intensity of past trauma without becoming emotionally overwhelmed. By using bodymind awareness, rigid or chaotic extremes can be shifted to more *integrated* functioning through engaging in active release.

Somatic Experiencing (SE) therapy[3] offers an array of body-based tools for the emotional expression of stored traumatic experiences. Focusing on our bodily actions, we can tap into stored trauma to engage in nervous system expression and release.

SE interventions generally involve direct attention to physical sensations, with the trauma story as only a backdrop. For example, a trauma victim whose arms and shoulders hold pain from a past experience of being restrained might work to gradually *integrate* awareness of these sensations by creating opportunities to extend her arms and expand the space she occupies—to "take back" her personal sense of power, thereby transitioning from "victim" to "survivor."

A somatic tool that can offer significant relief is making a deep vibrational sound to express and reconnect segments of the nervous system that have been isolated by stored trauma. In this practice, breath, sound vibrations, and muscles work together to *reintegrate* previously blocked channels of communication and expression, allowing access to *witnessing* and support.

Other bodymind tools to promote *integration* involve rhythmic motions to access resources across the right and left hemispheres of the brain—a process known as bilateral stimulation, which is essential to mastery of important developmental processes such as coordination and balance.

*****

Connecting with and expanding opportunities for bodymind *integration* are effective ways to support and sustain recovery. By participating in activities of movement and Self-expression, we can extend and enrich our FLOWING recovery.

Notes

1. Daniel J. Siegel, *Pocket Guide to Interpersonal Neurobiology: An Integrative Handbook of the Mind* (New York: Norton, 2012), 16–17.

2. Ibid.

3. Peter A. Levine, *In an Unspoken Voice: How the Body Releases Trauma and Restores Goodness* (Berkeley, CA: North Atlantic Books, 2010).

Living through trauma is a transformative experience.
How will you grow from grief and loss?

nine

NURTURE: CONNECTING FLOWING

Magical Minnesota Journey

After attending our niece's wedding, Elliott and I, along with our sons, daughter-in-law and grandson, set out on the two-hour drive north to our family cabin. We spent the next five days at the cabin in our usual way: taking long walks, enjoying campfires, reading, and playing board games. Although the seasonal change limited our time on the lake, every day was warm and sunny.

Being together as a family was a joy, although the activity level in the small space was challenging. Between that and the unfamiliar, too-small bed, I slept poorly and suffered from joint pain. I suspected that the damage from my chemotherapy had come back to haunt me in the form of overactive nerve endings and aching joints. I tried to check in with my Parts, but in the crowded cabin it was hard to make clear, uninterrupted contact.

* * * * *

When my family left at the week's end, I remained at the cabin to write. I confessed to myself some fear at the new experience of being alone in a somewhat isolated northern woodland in the dark of the night, with only the dog for company. But

I didn't allow my fears to stop me. On that first morning, I pushed the big oak table up to the picture window overlooking the lake and dragged the extra chairs into unused rooms to minimize clutter. A rocking chair that I pulled into the cabin from the deck offered a surprisingly comfortable spot for reading and contemplation. And sweeping and mopping the floors allowed me to start afresh in my now-private retreat.

I wrote in my journal and then moved down to the dock with my yoga mat for my daily stretch—the sounds of the lake, the wind, and classical piano music playing through open cabin windows creating a soothing backdrop.

After my lakeside stretch and meditation, I climbed into a hammock to read a new book I'd discovered back home: The Art of Everyday Ecstasy.[1] *I started reading where the book opened at random to a chapter on creating meaningful ritual—realizing that was exactly what I'd been doing as I cleaned and arranged my space for the week of writing and contemplation ahead. I laughed out loud before settling in to consider how to use the ideas to create a memorial for my recently departed sister when my remaining siblings joined me the following week.*

* * * * *

Newly inspired, I set out for a walk with my border collie, Kaya, who suddenly seemed younger and more nimble than she had in years. The autumn colors were at their best in the bright northern sunlight, with shadows slanting from the low apex of the sun's course across the sky. Kaya showed me where to go and told me when it was time to turn back.

On return, I felt guided to prepare a campfire in a little lakeside pit. I dragged a dead branch from one of the pines that my grandmother had planted decades earlier to the circle of rocks. Having no hatchet, I broke sections off the trunk by stomping on it while it rested on the edge of a stone bench.

Hot and satisfied with my efforts, I walked down to the lake and dunked myself in the chilly waters, letting my internal "little girl" twirl with joy at the sense of adventure and Self-energy. Then, as I'd done happily each year since childhood, I waded along the shore, collecting granite and quartz stones worn smooth from the sand.

I let my swimsuit dry as I watched the sunset from the dock, then changed into my jeans and went back out to light the fire. I took the time to honor the four directions of the compass and to thank Mother Earth for the fuel I burned as daylight faded. After going inside to enjoy a candle-lit dinner, I returned to the dock with Kaya and watched the stars for an hour. Then, back in the cabin, I locked the windows and doors, and closed the outer curtains, keeping on minimal lights so I could see the twinkling stars reflected on the lake before drifting off to sleep.

The next day, the weather was cooler thanks to a brief overnight storm, making it easier for me to stay inside to write. After my day of transition and ritual, all things seemed possible in that place of unfolding. Ancestors who had come before me shared the space with me as I wrote from their inspiration and silently thanked them for their gifts.

* * * * *

The next week, I welcomed my remaining siblings to the cabin where we'd spent so many childhood summers. We reconnected with each other and with the spirit of the place. On the day before my drive home, we sang old songs and created little paper boats from the leftover funeral programs featuring our elder sister's beautiful smiling image. Her spirit present among us, each of us wrote a message to her as we shared in our sibling energy. At sunset, we lit the boats and released them to the windswept lake, inviting our departed sister to join our ancestors in that magical place.

The answers to your questions can only be found inside.

To sustain *integration* and strengthen healthy functioning, we must make opportunities to *nurture* our recovery practice—to support our healing through regular engagement with newly discovered Self-energy. Among the best ways to sustain recovery are practicing small personal rituals and participating in meaningful celebrations.

BENEFITS OF RITUALS AND CELEBRATIONS

By making the everyday sacred, rituals *nurture* our recovery. Frequent moments for awareness arise if only we take time to look at the meaning in small, daily tasks. Engaging with "ordinary miracles"—the ticking sound of a warming tea kettle, the crunch of leaves during a walk through the woods, or the sight of children at play, for example—allows us to connect through our physical and emotional senses to the positive energies in our environment.

By making the everyday sacred,
rituals nurture *our recovery.*

Even more beneficial is to expand day-to-day activities—even tasks like doing the laundry or taking clean dishes out of the dishwasher and putting them away—into clearly marked, meaning-filled rituals. (After all, aren't such routine actions, at their heart, expressions of our love for order, spaciousness, and predictability?) Furthermore, celebrating important events—the achievement of milestones such as meeting a personal goal or completing a project, for example—can invest them with greater meaning and extend their magic.

If we celebrate our achievements as well as seeking support in times of loss, there is a natural process of FLOWING across relationships. Each encounter strengthens the bonds between, and the flexibility of recovery resources among, those connected around the event. Instead of withholding our gains and our pains for fear of creating disappointments or inconveniences, we can share our energies, taking turns at being the supporter or the one being supported in an endless series of celebrations and markers of loss—benefiting all.

Many rituals are offered for release from struggles or to let go of unwanted negative energy or old habits that no longer serve us. Release options can take the form of sensory expression, using the voice, vision, touch, sound, and movement; or the release can be symbolic or meaning driven as guided by intention, awareness, activity, and expression. Some ceremonies are object focused, using a talisman chosen from nature or history, or a newly created item can be crafted or discovered in one's environment. Our society's most *nurturing* practices are relational, demonstrating curiosity, compassion, permission, and mutual respect of one another.

Our society's most nurturing *practices demonstrate curiosity, compassion, permission, and mutual respect of one another.*

Engagement in such powerful meaning-making can help promote recovery by highlighting positive experiences to counter past negative ones. By repeating practices and experiences that you have adopted as your personal rituals, you can *nurture* positive change, using your brain's neuroplasticity to support your recovery. All that's necessary is for you to decide to invest in the life-changing potential of otherwise ordinary moments.

ELEMENTS OF RITUAL

The only real requirements of rituals are intention, preparation, enactment, and closing.

As a young girl, I could hardly contain my excitement around birthdays and holidays, but somehow they never seemed to measure up to my expectations. When I was older, the enthusiasm was dampened by what I now understand to be protective internal Parts that kept me from risking disappointment.

I see that same sort of risk aversion on a larger scale among the trauma survivors with whom I work. Often, they seemingly set themselves up by avoiding contact or refusing to let others know about upcoming anniversaries or special events. In doing so, however, disappointments are actually enhanced, transformed into something more like betrayal, and negative patterns become self-fulfilling prophecies of hurt and isolation. Opportunities for connection and acknowledgment are surrendered, amounting to losses for not just the individual, but an entire support system.

After my experience of cancer treatment, my family and I held a big "Forty and Feeling Fine" birthday party. I knew my friends needed closure on that difficult time as much as I did because they were similarly affected by the experience of fear and potential loss.

That party marked a change in my habitual guarded approach of downplaying milestones. My new, post-party attitude became "celebrate every chance you get!" I decided to regularly acknowledge the importance of each moment and to emphasize *presence over presents* by inviting others to both participate in my meaningful moments and to share theirs with me. Such strengthened bonds are the greater purpose of connecting through meaningful ritual.

Establishing Intention

An intention to begin the day by engaging positive energy can develop into one or more flexible forms of ritual to support *nurturing*. Setting aside time to calm the mind—whether stepping out in your back yard to sit among the trees and birdsong, driving to a meditation center, arranging flowers, or lighting incense—can create the space needed for effective ritual practice.

Making a clear statement of *intention* will guide the *form* of your ritual practice. A statement of intention may be as simple as vocalizing a word or phrase like "clarity" or "opening to experience." This statement, when combined with significant activities such as lighting a candle or stepping into a sacred circle, can offer powerful *nurturing* to your recovery efforts.

Intentionally connecting to the present moment and celebrating one's natural access to healing is a sacred act. Sacred means "holy" and implies wholeness. With intention and awareness, we can create our own "sacred spaces" to support our recovery.

Many people find meaning and support for their spiritual access within the structure of conventional religions, but opportunities to access the "divine spark" within and between each of us need not be limited to temples, chapels, or mosques.

To *nurture* the active elements of FLOWING, it is necessary to hold such sacred spaces in our life. Taking time out from ringing cell phones and busy schedules is not luxury; it is key to emotional and physical health.

Taking time out from ringing cell phones and busy schedules is key to emotional and physical health.

Since few of us have time for extended retreats on a regular basis, small daily celebrations of Self-access must be found within and between our regularly scheduled activities. So instead of struggling to trek across town to find a calm sacred environment, look for opportunities to build "little altars everywhere"[2] and to create meaning and ritual wherever you are.

With focused intention, even the simplest activity can take on dignity and powerful expression of meaning, enhancing our engagement with our world and contributing to recovery.

Preparing for Ritual

Most of us have daily practices or rituals of preparation and action. A morning shower begins with a certain amount of routine that is part efficiency, part self-care. With intention and some preparation, daily routines can become meaningful moments of celebration. Those minor moments can be added to and expanded with a bit of effort, establishing a strong foundation for flexible coping by *nurturing* our recovery.

Taking time to set up the space for your ritual practice by bringing in positive energy can be an important beginning to the process. Celebrating in nature, opening windows to allow fresh air, or using essential oils or (if it can be done safely) "smudging" with a bundle of white sage either before or as a part of the ritual, are among the many ways to cleanse stale or negative energies.

Planning ahead will offer opportunity to raise the level of meaning of your ritual through gathering the elements to be used. Consider the purpose of the activity, review your statement of intention, and then gather and plan the use of sacred items in your ceremony.

Planning ahead will offer opportunity to raise the level of meaning of your ritual through gathering the elements to be used.

Rituals can form around representational objects—for example, an item that recalls fond memories such as mom's favorite mug for morning tea—or an item from nature such as a rock or shell that recalls a treasured vacation spot. Ritual also can be engaged through sensory contact, such as filling a bowl with water and blossoms, or lighting a scented candle, to make the process tangible.

Other preparations may include the effort and choice to participate in a group and to connect with others. Even simple things like greetings and conversations, sharing tea and sometimes a meal, and inquiring about jobs and families are opportunities in that they *nurture*, expand, and *integrate* our internal and external connections. Therefore, as you prepare your ritual, decide who will be invited to participate, and perhaps ask them to join in the planning process as well.

By showing up and being mindful of and with one another, we engage a whole universe of new opportunities within every moment. Whether in a formal practice space, a casual meeting with a friend, or sitting quietly and looking inward, we can celebrate connection. When we prepare for a ritual, there is unlimited opportunity in life to *nurture* each and all on their own spiritual journey of creative recovery.

Enacting Ritual

The entire sequence of a ritual may last only the time of a mindful breath; or the ritual can be engaged and structured in a longer, more formal practice with multiple elements, activities, or participants. In either case, marking the beginning and end of the ritual, at least briefly, can make taking on the new task seem less daunting and ultimately more meaningful.

The enactment of your ritual can take place across a variety of levels including physical (chakra, body awareness), spatial (a building, room, or garden), temporal (anniversary, change of seasons), or direction driven (compass, heaven and earth). It could be structured around a desired outcome, perhaps representing the intended result, but without attachment to a particular manifestation of that result. Think in terms of "best outcome" rather than "it has to be exactly as I picture it."

As part of enacting the ritual, a clear expression of gratitude and intention will fully engage the bodymind in the practice. Surrendering the intention to a greater power, with an awareness of the limitations of our control over outcome, elevates the ritual to spiritual expression. Once a ceremony or ritual is enacted, it takes on its own significance. It is no longer "our" ritual but instead an event that goes beyond any particular agenda. By releasing the outcome to whatever forces of energy or spirit may be engaged with it, you show faith in the universe.

Blocked energies need to be *felt*, acknowledged, and released to correct imbalances and allow healing. Trauma is one significant type of toxin requiring release, but there are many sources across the bodymind energy spectrum. Disruptions of such energies might be caused by emotional, social, or environmental challenges. Release of those blocked energies is necessary to allow *integration*.

Closing Ritual Elements

Careful attention to closing and either putting away or holding the ritual elements, depending on their purpose, will maintain meaning across time and serve as a reminder of the continuance of intention through regular practice. Try to plan a specific ending activity and establish an intention to follow through with what you started. This may mean clearing elements of the ritual or establishing a display area or shrine for ongoing intentions. You might set a reminder to take a time to periodically reengage with the ritual, or some aspect of it, to further the *nurturing* qualities of your intention.

—m—

Plan a specific ending activity and establish and intention to follow through.

—m—

Be flexible, have fun, and bring creativity to your practice of ritual. If it becomes a chore, you'll be less likely to return to this opportunity for mindful expression with any regularity, missing out on the *integrative* benefits of regular practice. (See the end of this chapter for ideas and elements to include in building ritual.)

—⁂—

Be flexible, have fun, and bring creativity to your practice of ritual.

—⁂—

EXPANDING RITUAL

Our environment is affected by industrial waste, our attention disturbed by a million disruptions, and our relationships distorted by multiple factors of personality and coping styles. In small doses, our nervous systems can assimilate and recover from such disruptions, but in ever more complex combinations such toxins can compromise our immune system and ability to cope with stress.[3]

To counter such overloaded and blocked energy, it is helpful to cultivate meaningful expressive rituals, perhaps on a broader, community-based level. We are surrounded by news of suffering in our community and in our world. These many challenges to our security and well-being can have cumulative effects, increasing our tendency to withdraw in self-protective ways.

As will be considered in the next chapter, engaging with others to make a better world is an opportunity to expand our healing efforts. Moving from personal to communal to global healing is a natural extension of the FLOWING model.

Holding to the concept that, in the long run, we are all one in a vast network of connection is essential to the larger meaning of *nurturing* in recovery.

* * * * *

Focus and intention are what give ritual practices their power, not the performance of any particular activity. Through these efforts and other opportunities to engage with the energy of the Self, with our community, and with our world, we can *nurture* and extend our FLOWING health and well-being.

Notes

1. Margot Anand, *The Art of Everyday Ecstasy: The Seven Tantric Keys for Bringing Passion, Spirit and Joy into Every Part of Your Life* (New York: Broadway Books, 1999).

2. Rebecca Wells, *Little Altars Everywhere* (New York: Harper Collins, 1992).

3. Andrew Weil, MD, *Spontaneous Healing: How to Discover and Enhance Your Body's Natural Ability to Maintain and Heal Itself* (New York: Knopf, 1995).

RITUAL RESOURCES

REPRESENTATION

Elemental Rites:

- **Fire**
  Candles
  Sunlight
  Fireplace

- **Earth**
  Sand/Soil/Rocks
  Wood/Leaves
  Plants/Herbs/Dried Flowers
  Ceramic/Glass/Metal

- **Water**
  Fountains/Pools
  Lake/Bowl/Still Water
  Stream/Shower/ Moving Water
  Bath/Puddles
  Waterfall/Rain

- **Air**
  Breath
  Mist
  Smoke
  Incense

ENGAGEMENT

- **Senses**
  Sight
  Sound
  Scent
  Touch
  Taste
  Intuition

- **Activity**
  Imagery
  Movement
  Breathing
  Mindfulness
  Meditation
  Song
  Mantra
  Poetry

- **Events**
  Milestones
  Seasons
  Decisions
  Losses
  Accomplishments

Generations of meanings and connections are carried within and between us. We can choose what to pass on and what to release.

ten

GENERATE: FLOWING OUTWARD

Full Circle

I was free and clear, sixteen years after my cancer diagnosis—or was I? A hard lump had emerged on my sternum and ribs, tied to my reconstructed breast. It was wedge-shaped, exactly at the center of my heart-space. It must have been building up for some time—just one aspect of the spiraling pressure on my spine from so many displaced and repaired body parts—but its sudden expansion took me by surprise.

My initial response, a casual sort of denial, was that it was probably just a spot of calcification. But then I experienced sudden, middle-of-the-night panic that it might be something more sinister—a result of the much-dreaded radiation beams that had burned flesh in that very location. I tried to approach the problem calmly, first with phone calls, then visits, and then procedures separated by unavoidable but nerve-wracking delays. The results were negative, but I was encouraged at each step to take the next one "just in case." All the while, the little wedge continued to expand its territory.

I turned my compassion and attention toward my little alien visitor, willing it to be kind to our body in return. When the ultrasound view led to a biopsy, it was time for me to look deeply into my own reserves. I sorted through the possible outcomes and felt profound gratitude for the gifts received over the years of recovery. I was aware of feeling a proven sense of quiet peace during the time between the biopsy and the report of results.

* * * * *

The "all-clear" gave me immense relief, but surgery was nonetheless suggested as a cautionary measure. As these events were unfolding, I noticed increasing discomfort in my neck and left shoulder. Physical and emotional preoccupations caused my energy level to falter. The lump was now visible in the mirror, no longer merely palpable by touch. I redoubled my newly refined mindfulness skills to keep my body calm and control my fear of yet another painful procedure and convalescence.

The surgery went smoothly, and I had minimal pain from the incision. But my body's response to the anesthetic was extreme. During the first three days, the nausea and migraine reminded me of the struggles of chemotherapy years earlier. But even in the midst of the pain, I was aware that the tightness in my shoulder had loosened. As my recovery unfolded over the next few days, I had a continuing sense of letting go of something I hadn't realized I was holding. My balance felt more secure, and I could breathe more freely.

At my post-op consultation, the surgeon confirmed that the old tether to my core—the abdominal muscle that had been used to form the breast—had been severed in removal of the fibrous tissue. The damaged area of tissue had advanced to the point that it crouched directly on my ribs, a solid block of scar constricting my heart-space. Now that it was gone, I discovered that its absence felt luxurious and energizing. I felt more at home in my body and discovered movement away from some of my emotional reactivity to old losses. I found myself releasing some of the self-protective restrictions that I had relied on in the past and more comfortable expressing my Self without fear of rejection.

* * * * *

It occurred to me that my body's own wisdom had isolated and eventually demanded removal of those blocks, in the process reminding me of pain and fear from years earlier. The opening of my heart-space allowed energy to flow into personal as well as physical healing. I recognized the path of review, resource, and release that underlies all recovery. And yet again, I was awed and appreciative of the bodymind's inherent wisdom and the profoundly humbling experience of another unkind gift.

We are always becoming.

Finding the way home to Self after experiencing trauma and loss is an ongoing journey. New challenges arise and require us to retrace our steps to pick up where we may have lost the trail. This review of earlier efforts is not a sign of failure but instead an opportunity to reinforce and expand our resources to make them even more durable.

As we grow stronger in our sense of competence at recovery, we have something new to share. There is no better way to reinforce our own learning than to teach it to another, no better way to appreciate a gift than to share it with others.

There is no better way to appreciate a gift than to share it with others.

GENERATIVITY

The term *generativity* was introduced by social psychologist Erik Erikson to describe engagement in a meaningful, contributive way during one's later years of life.[1] This concept of continued creative process—of engaging with the unavoidable challenges of aging and loss in a way that adds value—is a powerful one. It is a defining opportunity to make our time on this earth purposeful: a legacy to future *generations* and an open-ended commitment to adding positive energy by our FLOWING recovery.

Generativity is supported through compassionate interactions with others. The starting point for such interactions must be to *open* our heart-space—actively inviting engagement from a nonjudgmental perspective and expressing that *openness* to others. The heart, an essential organ whose symbolic significance is as the emotional source of love, is truly the ultimate *generator.*

—≈—

The heart is truly
the ultimate generator.

—≈—

Creative engagement with the challenges of survival is essential to directing our efforts at *generativity.* Every new moment is a creative act and every interaction an opportunity to expand the influence of FLOWING in the world. Positive exchanges may project themselves into the life and relationships of each person we meet. Failures of connection or negative reactions may block or subvert those energies, becoming opportunities lost.

Engaging in a *generative* way is expansive. As we *listen* with curiosity and respect, we create opportunities for participating in community in meaningful ways. When we access and unburden our Parts, energies are freed up to allow connection with others. Instead of being isolated by protective coping, we meet with friends, consider new perspectives and expand awareness of our place in the world.

Compassion is by its very nature a state of receptivity to those around us, so we find resonance with the suffering and the joys of others. With regular and intentional practice, we bear *witness* to suffering and send forth energy that may offer relief or healing to those whom we cannot reach directly. Even further, we can *nurture* a sense of community to build our intentions into actions that may create a groundswell of change.

Finding an arena in which you can participate in the healing of others will advance that cause on personal, interpersonal, and even global levels. Opportunities to share in healing exchanges can be as gentle as holding mental space to consider the needs of a loved one or as active as engaging in community advancement around a cause that is dear to your heart.

We all heal best in interpersonal relationships—in brain-to-brain engagement and presence with purpose. Finding opportunity to engage with others in a common effort through volunteerism and participation is a strong example of the practice of *generativity* as well as generosity. Bringing an *open* heart to your engagement with others can change the world, one interaction at a time.

GENERATIONAL RECOVERY

Our sense of identity is powerfully influential in the scheme of who we are as citizens of the world and as partners in relationships. Those lines of meaning-filled energy from ages past are rooted in our ancestry. These immeasurable forces contribute sometimes subtle, other times vast energies that guide our efforts and focus in life.

Genealogy is most often traced through paternal lines, but patterns of emotional influence tend to be carried through the maternal lineage. In the past, mothers may not have held property rights, but they held responsibility for the early care of their children. While fathers managed the things of the outside world, those relating to safety and shelter, it was more likely the mothers who reflected their felt sense of living in the world, including their own and their children's places in it. These maternal ancestral influences are less about name and position, more about perspectives passed along, just as certainly as blood type and chromosomes. They develop over time and *generations* as cultural, familial, and personally unique expressions of identity.

In my office, within arms' reach of a chair that was once my mother's and is now my favorite spot to sit while writing, is a large cabinet—a wardrobe of adventures of family members who came before me. The stories, dates, and artifacts held in this wardrobe belong to generations of my lineage—an extended kinship that can be traced to the Norman Conquest and earlier, into mists of time. There is direct transmission to me through genetics, stories shared, recorded history, and items collected and protected by archivists who were also my kin—a multitude of layers of meaning and intention, filtered by time and collected in one cabinet.

From my comfortable writing chair, I have a direct view of the aged catalpa tree outside. The protective branches of this "grandfather tree" shield our home from sun and storms, and its extended roots ground me into deepest earth. The wardrobe, comfy chair, and gnarled old tree are living history, rooted deep in time and space with open-ended potential for transference of energy to an unknown future. Whenever I sit at their meeting place, my bodymind is ready to receive what is carried in their interwoven influences.

GENETIC EXPRESSION

Generativity resonates across interpersonal interactions, *generations*, cultures, and even our genetic expression. Researchers have discovered that exposure to trauma creates genetic changes that are encoded and passed on through multiple subsequent *generations* by a process called epigenesis. Further explorations indicate that mindfulness practices are epigenetically healing. These are examples of adaptations that further our options for the survival of the species in a changing world.

—∿—

Exposure to trauma creates genetic changes that are encoded and passed on through multiple subsequent generations.

—∿—

Maintaining our recovery through engagement in FLOWING *generativity* leads to greater well-being in the bodymind. The healing response that exists within each of us can be accessed in the course of *integration*, through incremental changes that have immediate effects. Lifestyle changes like stress management and nutritional interventions have been found to change genetic expressions within a few days. Age- and disease-related telomeres—the fragile tips at the ends of chromosome strands in our DNA—can be supported to increase flexibility in our immune responses. Secondary influences can be noted in the microbiome of gut bacteria within minutes to hours, and if sustained, will positively influence genetic expression.[2]

Gene expression has been compared to a piano keyboard: the keys are limited in number, but in combination, they can produce endless variations of sound. It is clear that the choices we make within our life "compositions" can have profound and lasting effects.

A different approach to the understanding of *generativity* comes from biologist Rupert Sheldrake. Sheldrake writes about the concept of morphogenic fields as an explanation of how individual experiences can mutually influence people, species, and natural systems across vast distances and time periods.

He describes these fields as energies that are carried within the very cells of every organism:

> The fields organizing the activity of the nervous system are...inherited through morphic resonance, conveying a collective, instinctive memory. Each individual both draws upon and contributes to the collective memory of the species. This means that new patterns of behavior can spread more rapidly than would otherwise be possible....Through morphic resonance, the patterns of activity in self-organizing systems are influenced by similar patterns in the past, giving each species and each kind of self-organizing system a collective memory.[3]

This resonance affects the way we are influenced by our shared familial and cultural inheritance, as well as how the unique qualities and experiences of individual interactions can be expressed across interpersonal relationships, even at great distances. This unseen web of connections highlights the influence of significant relationships on our sense of Self. Further, it offers support to our understanding of the collective nature of human experience and for the potential effectiveness of applying the FLOWING model of recovery for internal, interpersonal, and even universal resonance in expanding fields of *generativity*.

PROMOTING GLOBAL HEALING

To *generate* means to extend beyond what currently exists. Engagement with and dedication to our own recovery naturally affects those with whom we interact. It sets an example, encourages, inspires, and even changes the physiology of our loved ones as we engage them with compassion.

Our interconnected nature makes it essential to consider the influence we have on others and their influence on us. Parenting, friendships, and other relationships become programmed in our minds and hearts as aspects of our identity. With compassionate engagement, we extend our own energies to benefit others.

At times, the familiarity of present circumstances offers a sense of security that is hard to find in our limited view of what recovery could be like. When we find the theater of our relationships continually playing out the same show of hurt and rejection, we can either run from the pain through isolation and blame or engage with and *witness* the lasting influence of old hurts in order to promote healing and *generate* compassion.

The FLOWING model of recovery is an idea based in the belief that there is an inherent plan to life, and to human development. That plan is at the heart of our very being, but we tend to veer away when something blocks the road. As we clear that road of trauma-based obstacles, the route can be "recalculated" to guide us back to our inborn path.

Through recovery, disruptions are addressed and choices made based on what best resonates with us as newly *integrated* beings. Our *open*-hearted engagement can be the spark that ignites recovery and healing in those around us.

As we take on the tasks of personal recovery, it becomes possible to *generate* new meanings in our lives and to offer healing examples and support to our community. Mindful engagement in such effort is the key to personal change, which—like a pebble thrown in a lake—can have a ripple effect far beyond our immediate circle of interpersonal influence. In this manner, our recovery becomes not just a gift to ourselves but a gift to the expanding universe and to *generations* beyond our own.

Though our shared travels are at an end, your journey is just getting started. The unique form and direction of your FLOWING path are there for you to discover through your own curiosity and Self-leadership.

Notes

1. Erik H. Erikson, *Identity: Youth and Crisis* (New York: Norton, 1968).

2. Christine Tara Peterson, Vandana Sharma, Lisa Elmén, and Scott N. Peterson, "Immune Homeostasis, Dysbiosis and Therapeutic Modulation of the Gut Microbiota," *Clinical and Experimental Immunology* 197, no. 3 (October 2014): 363–77.

3. Rupert Sheldrake, *Morphic Resonance: The Nature of Formative Causation* (Rochester, VT: Park Street Press, 2009).

Your journey is just getting started.

APPENDIX A
Special Topics for Professionals

As therapists, how do we begin to cross the barriers of mistrust and self-blame that often protect trauma victims from the huge risk of being "seen" and cared about by another?

For victims, the early months of treatment are like a tug of war between the need for human connection and the learned experience of betrayal that is a hallmark of trauma. Whether the traumatic event was a natural disaster, a life-threatening health crisis, intentional harm by another person, or any other emotion-charged experience, the damage to their ability to trust is long lasting.

Honesty is critical to the development of any therapeutic relationship—exponentially so when we are trying to forge a relationship with a trauma survivor. Our ability to be clear about the terms of the treatment contract and to gently share our belief in the healing capacity of human beings—even in the aftermath of profound loss—is fundamental to being able to establish even the most basic working relationship with a trauma victim.

Such a position will ring false not deeply held. Moreover, as therapists, we must be prepared for our optimistic view of the potential for healing to be challenged by our clients. Trauma victims, after all, see life at its darkest and may try to convince supporters of the naiveté of optimism. Yet hope, of course, is at the center of all successful recovery efforts.

SURVIVOR, HEAL THYSELF (FIRST)

The greatest hazard we encounter in our jobs as therapists is blurring or even substituting our personal issues with those of our clients. There is a fine line between our essential task of boundary management and that of attending to *resonance within our Self*—the most powerful means of accessing true connection with a client and supporting real recovery. This is especially so in trauma work, because our personal experience fuels and deepens our understanding of survivors' stories of fear and loss.

Even though every story of trauma is unique, there is comfort for any client in knowing that a caring other—the therapist—has also experienced personal challenges and survived. That someone else has blazed a trail through like pain, experienced similar gut-wrenching feelings, and fought the good fight of recovery is living proof for a trauma victim that losses *can* be recovered from. And sharing such a message with a trauma victim—while maintaining the focus on the victim's personal recovery—goes a long way toward giving us the credibility we need to guide these clients through an extended recovery process.

Indeed, full engagement with our clients demands that we access a deep level of personal vulnerability.[1] But by our very exposure to a client's deepest pain, we inevitably take on some of that pain. It is a double-edged sword, but there is a way we can protect ourselves from its sharp edge and avoid secondary trauma in our personal lives.

It is critical for us to monitor and express this burden so as to maintain our own FLOWING process and serve as conduit, not a container, for a client's release of personal trauma burdens. To neglect our essential self-care is to allow ourselves to hold onto, accumulate, and create blocks within our own internal system, risking damage to ourselves, including burnout and the loss of our ability to work effectively as professionals.[2]

SETTING AND MAINTAINING THERAPEUTIC BOUNDARIES

Given their past histories of boundary violations of abuse and other trauma-based experiences, it is no surprise that clients may carry their boundary confusion into the treatment relationship—in the form of dismissive and mistrusting rejection of therapy, demands for more support, or inappropriate overtures toward intimacy. I frequently hear stories of therapists, psychiatrists, and physicians who terminated their professional relationship with a client whose inappropriate or unrealistic expectations and treatment-compromising demands undermined their therapy.

Because the pitfalls of mismanaging therapeutic boundaries are so significant, each of us in a healing profession must have a clear policy for addressing boundary clarification. In addition, we must be prepared to confront boundary violations without completing a client's self-fulfilling prophesy of abandonment.

Such relationship patterns are part and parcel of the repetitive cycle of trauma burdens in need of *integration*. The therapy relationship is nearly always subject to the replaying of disrupted relationship dynamics, especially so in the case of trauma therapy. The greatest hope for our trauma clients' healing is in our ability to bring them to a more flexible completion of those dynamics—and clear, consistent boundaries are essential to that task.

ADDRESSING TRAUMA BONDS

Even the most dangerous of family environments feels to a trauma victim like a safer alternative than the unknowns of the outside world. Later in life, the victim is still likely to place value in this bond and to feel disloyal in rethinking or reworking those early relationships. It therefore may be useful to encourage traumatized individuals and families, especially those with severe attachment disruptions, to adopt a broader perspective on family loyalty, suggesting that negative familial transmission patterns *indicate blocked energies on a multigenerational scale.*[3] Other useful approaches are helping clients recall and celebrate (sometimes rare) indications of appropriate parenting effort, and recommending that the client view these as glimmers of the parent's *true Self* peeking through the accumulation of damaging interactions. In this way, rather than adhering to the commandment to "honor thy mother and thy father"—complete with the traumatizing behaviors—clients can seek their caregivers' highest purpose: bringing a child to maturity through difficult times.

With this new perspective comes the possibility of recovery by investing in opportunities to heal the family. Though challenging for clients to *integrate* after years of negative communications, the prospect of reaching their potential and accessing healing for the family system as a whole is compelling.

Of course, continued attention to safety remains paramount to the trauma victim's ability to avoid potential revictimization within established relationship patterns. Trauma survivors therefore must be encouraged to be vigilant so as not to fall into old interactional patterns and dysfunctional family dynamics.

RECOGNIZING AND ADDRESSING EMOTIONAL NEEDS

At the front line of trauma care are the doctors and nurses who treat injuries and bind the physical wounds of trauma victims. These dedicated professionals are generally trained at offering services to patients in a "body-first" manner—as it should be in life-or-death situations. But such a view risks creating among trauma victims the misimpression that they are viewed as less than a whole person. For this reason, once the physical crisis has been attended to, it is important to shift the focus to the victim's emotional and psychological injuries.

The many faces of trauma require a multipronged approach to exploration and recovery. Failure to expand the field of attention to broader relational issues can allow emotional and psychological injuries to fester. To further support recovery efforts, it may be worthwhile for medical personnel to collaborate with, or refer to, psychotherapists and other complementary healing professionals who are skilled in somatic and body work therapies—which can powerfully increase opportunities for trauma victims to release blockages and limit the toxic effects of extreme stress.[4]

COMPLEMENTARY APPROACHES TO HEALING

Great strides in healing often can be found among "complementary" and alternative approaches. There are many effective applications of alternative therapies, including approaches to manage anxiety and physical discomfort, reinforce immune processes, and improve general well-being.[5] Also, many complementary practices have been researched and proven effective for personal mastery of emotions and improved immune response, thus demonstrating their valuable place in the treatment regimen.

It is important for the support team (medical, psychological, and social) to view helping trauma sufferers find the best options for healing as part of their "job description." The greatest benefit to offering survivors a range of options is in the increased sense of choice that the mere fact of having options creates within a survivor's otherwise generally uncontrolled experience of trauma.

PROVIDING CALM, STEADY SUPPORT

Trauma work is about developmental repair. Even traumas known to be from adult experience impact the survivor at a deep level of meaning. It can be confusing for a therapist to see survivors function well and logically understand so much of their experiences, yet continue to be reactive and impractical in their responses. To push beyond a survivor's current level of *integration*, however, will only increase the patient's anxiety and work counter to therapeutic goals.

Staying calm and steady in your support of the recovery is the only way to reach the treatment goals you have established with the patient. Watch for minor developmental gains and indications of flexibility—small steps that can signal a shift toward the enhanced *integration* on which a solid foundation of true recovery must be built. This is the great reward for your endurance, and it may yield some of the most powerful gifts to be offered within your chosen life's work.

Notes

1. Richard C. Schwartz, *Introduction to the Internal Family Systems Model* (Oak Park, IL: Trailheads Publication, 2001).

2. Laura van Dernoot Lipsky and Connie Burk, *Trauma Stewardship: An Everyday Guide to Caring for Self While Caring for Others* (San Francisco: Barrett-Koehler, 2009).

3. Christine A. Courtois and Julian D. Ford, *Treating Complex Traumatic Stress Disorders: An Evidence-Based Guide* (New York: Guilford, 2009).

4. Peter A. Levine, *In an Unspoken Voice: How the Body Releases Trauma and Restores Goodness* (Berkeley, CA: North Atlantic Books, 2010).

5. Andrew Weil, *Spontaneous Healing: How to Discover and Enhance Your Body's Natural Ability to Maintain and Heal Itself* (New York: Knopf, 1995).

APPENDIX B

Facing Trauma Together: Guidance for Family Members and Other Nonprofessional Partners

Traumatic injuries tend to block emotional development. There is no way around those blocks, so the survivor must find the way through them. Having to revisit painful past events can be daunting; after all, these experiences were too much to handle in the first place. And making matters even worse, the energy that the survivor spends on avoiding memories of the past makes the trauma seem even more overwhelming.

It takes great resolve for survivors to make their way back through the experience of loss to engage the healing process. And even the best therapy will benefit from a support system characterized by a strong commitment to relationship-based healing.[1] Indeed, trauma recovery is most effective with the involvement of a consistently supportive partner. A "secure base"—whether a spouse, a best friend, a family member, or a support group—will allow the survivor the safety from which to explore and resolve the effects of the trauma.

The support role can be very difficult to maintain in the face of a victim's loyalty challenges and demands based in distorted projections from the original trauma.

At times, it may seem to supporters that their best efforts are met only with demanding behavior and "relational sabotage" on the part of the trauma victim. Such behaviors—which often are indicators of the sort of betrayal the survivor experienced within the traumatic relationship—offer supporters an opportunity for resolution if addressed by establishing clear, compassionate boundaries.

FAMILY SYSTEMS IN TRAUMA

At their most fundamental level, families are environments of growth and development. Family teaches us who we are. As such, the family environment is highly influential to harm as well as healing. If the family environment was a source of harm in the past, the survivor can have great difficulty in moving toward recovery, which requires reconciling the "rules" learned about respect and loyalty to family members with past hurtful treatment. Negative patterns in troubled families can even set up feelings within a survivor of having deserved the abuse.

Without active efforts toward change, negative patterns may block options for the trauma victim's healing by limiting the self-awareness that is critical for recovery from illness and trauma. Family members may need to approach healing as a group effort, because if one member is hurting, all are likely affected. The sometimes painful truths of family dysfunction can be changed only by a commitment to healing in spite of existing "scripts" about family loyalties. This commitment may risk the loss of old alliances, but it offers the promise of a healthy future.

SUGGESTIONS FOR SUPPORTERS

Supporting a trauma victim demands acute self-awareness and may even require professional guidance through what can be a hazardous relationship journey. Consider the following suggestions for approaching the role of supporter or revising a supporter role you are now playing.

Tip 1: Work to Manage Boundaries

If you have made a commitment to truly help a trauma survivor, you will need strong boundaries to help you recognize when you are becoming overloaded and your own mental and physical health put at risk. Be willing to say no if you aren't comfortable with any aspect of your role but then be ready to help the survivor find alternative sources of support.

Tip 2: Practice Self-Care to Avoid Burnout

To sustain a supportive position in the life of a trauma victim and avoid burnout, it is essential for supporters to practice self-care and engage their own healing resources.[2] Finding options for personal expression will help you avoid getting caught up in the suffering of your traumatized partner. Exercising regularly, eating healthfully, getting enough sleep, and engaging in other healthy behaviors and activities are essential to the management of your own stress level.

Drawing water from a well that has gone dry is a good metaphor for burnout. To see your way through the trauma support role, to a time when the survivor can more readily manage independently, you must refill the well and flush the toxic level of exposure to another's suffering from your own system. Strong and silent may be an interesting character type in the movies, but your health and well-being in the midst of trauma work could easily be compromised by applying the same model. Just as the survivor must access opportunities for recovery, so should you look to the FLOWING model to move through the demanding role of support partner.

Tip 3: Make Connections

Supporters who feel they are "going it alone" risk falling into the same sense of hopelessness that can affect trauma survivors. To avoid isolation, survivors and supporters alike need access to a broad base of opportunity to engage with others. Through mentoring and support groups, survivors and supporters can make connections with others who are in similar circumstances, expand their emotional horizons, and promote personal healing.

Longtime supporters, even family members, may withdraw from contact with a trauma survivor due to their own feelings of vulnerability, perhaps even ending the survivor-supporter relationship—a phenomenon influenced by "anticipatory grieving."[3] In such circumstances, reaching out to connect with the broad array of available programs can be especially valuable.

Tip 4: Watch for Signs of Secondary PTSD

Secondary PTSD, also known as compassion fatigue, is ever a possibility for supporters and caregivers who exceed their personal limits.[4] The mechanism of trauma transmission is complex, but it is clear that the distorted perspectives of trauma survivorship have a contagious influence. At the first sign of secondary PTSD, seek out alternative sources of support and rely on your own self-care resources. Self-sacrifice in the face of another's suffering can lead only to further loss for both survivor and caregiver.

Tip 5: Debrief with a Professional

It is all too common for well-meaning supporters to attempt to take on the burden of supporting a loved one without sufficient tools for the task. Working with a trained professional is a great way to access essential information about trauma recovery, as well as to unload some of the burden you may carry as a result of your exposure to the suffering of your friend or loved one.

Tip 6: Look for the Rewards

Despite the difficulties of playing a supportive role in your traumatized loved one's recovery, the experience can be greatly rewarding. With attention to appropriate boundaries and your own self-care, you can find opportunities for personal growth and a strengthened bond with your friend or family member.

By looking toward the future to the recovery aspects of the partnership—rather than becoming bogged down in suffering—a new world of meaningful connection is within your reach. Seeking the gifts to be found in recovery from trauma can provide you and your partner with a shared journey of improved quality of life and the resiliency to take on whatever comes your way.

Notes

1. Diana Fosha, Daniel J. Siegel, and Marion F. Solomon, eds., *The Healing Power of Emotion: Affective Neuroscience, Development & Clinical Practice* (New York: Norton, 2009), 86–111.

2. Laura van Dernoot Lipsky, *Trauma Stewardship: An Everyday Guide to Caring for Yourself While Caring for Others* (San Francisco: Barrett-Koehler, 2009).

3. Dorothy S. Becvar, *In the Presence of Grief: Helping Family Members Resolve Death, Dying and Bereavement Issues* (New York: Guilford, 2001).

4. Charles Figley, ed., *Compassion Fatigue: Coping with Secondary Traumatic Stress Disorder in Those Who Treat the Traumatized* (New York: Brunner-Routledge, 1995).

INDEX